The Official Guide to

rootsweb.com

The Official Guide to

rootsweb.com

by Myra Vanderpool Gormley, CG
and Tana Pedersen Lord

ancestry publishing

Library of Congress Cataloging-in-Publication Data

Gormley, Myra Vanderpool, 1940-
 The official guide to RootsWeb.com / by Myra Vanderpool Gormley and Tana Pedersen Lord.
    p. cm.
 Includes bibliographical references and index.
 ISBN-13: 978-1-59331-309-8 (alk. paper)
 ISBN-10: 1-59331-309-8 (alk. paper)
 1. RootsWeb.com. 2. Genealogy—Computer network resources—Handbooks, manuals, etc.
 3. Internet research—Handbooks, manuals, etc. I. Pedersen Lord, Tana. II. Title.
 CS21.G67 2007
 929'.10285—dc22

                                                                                    2007009700

10 9 8 7 6 5 4 3 2 1
ISBN-13: 978-1-59331-309-8
ISBN-10: 1-59331-309-8

Printed in the United States of America.

Contents

Contents

Chapter 3

Getting the Most out of Message Boards 37

Introduction

Welcome to RootsWeb

RootsWeb traces its beginnings to the early days of the Internet. In the mid-eighties, net.roots, a genealogy newsgroup, attracted two young, recently graduated students, Brian Leverich and Karen Isaacson of California. In another part of the world, Alf Christophersen of Norway and Marty Hoag of North Dakota State University, created the first genealogy mailing list, ROOTS-L. The proverbial ball got rolling and within a few years a database of surnames (the RootsWeb Surname List) was created, and members of the ROOTS-L mailing list started making their own genealogy files available to each other over a network. Over the next decade, the World Wide Web was created and everyday people, not just computer-savvy experts, were online. In 1996, Karen and Brian officially registered the name of RootsWeb.com, and within the year they began accepting monetary contributions to keep the site going.

Then in June of 2000, MyFamily.com, Inc. (now The Generations Network, Inc.), owner of Ancestry.com, acquired RootsWeb; its support and funding has allowed the site to remain free to this day. From this original forum for genealogists to exchange e-mail via mailing lists, RootsWeb has grown into the largest grassroots genealogy community in the world with millions of family trees, mailing lists, databases, message boards, and Web pages—all submitted, maintained, and organized by family historians like you.

RootsWeb Today

Today, millions of family history enthusiasts all over the globe use RootsWeb to expand their research, share their accomplishments, contribute their genealogy files, and request help from fellow researchers. RootsWeb serves family historians of all interests—from those just starting their family search to professionals with years of experience. RootsWeb currently hosts the largest and most comprehensive collection of free genealogical resources available on the Internet. It provides interactive how-to guides, discussion lists, databases such as the Social Security Death Index, and numerous tools and search engines to help you learn more about your ancestors. Additionally, resources such as free Web space and message boards enable millions of researchers to find others who have similar interests or family connections. And, its weekly e-mail newsletter, the *RootsWeb Review,* is sent to subscribers around the world.

RootsWeb Tomorrow

RootsWeb will continue to grow as the worldwide genealogical community does. As technology provides additional ways to share and exchange information online, it will be the wants, wishes, and needs of family historians that

push the website forward into new frontiers. Development
of new search engines that make information easier to locate,
and tools that consolidate and better utilize older databases,
as well as reorganization of the site to simplify navigation
are major goals of the technical staff. However, for the most
part RootsWeb will always do what it does best—enable
genealogists to find and to share their information with others.

Regardless of whether you are a novice at tracing your
roots or an experienced professional, the sources and tools
available at RootsWeb can help you be successful in your
quest. While the major projects available at RootsWeb—
WorldConnect, mailing lists, message boards, and user-
contributed databases—are the most frequently used, there's
much more to be found at RootsWeb. Inside this book you will
discover more about RootsWeb and how to get the most out of
its sources and treasures.

Long-time Family Connections Revealed

By Virgie Morgan,
RootsWeb User

I have known my best friend, Mary, for more than twenty years. When she saw how wrapped up I was in tracing my family history and saw the success I was having at finding my ancestors, she became interested in searching for her ancestors as well.

So I began at RootsWeb, as I always do, and put her maiden name in the search engine. As we were going through the results, she suddenly spotted the names of her grandparents. We entered the database, confirmed that this was her family, and e-mailed the woman who owned the database. She was helpful in sharing her information.

My friend had not known anything about her father's side of the family and through this cousin she was able to finally know her father's people. We went as far as we could, and I created a family file for her on my *Family Tree Maker* program.

At Christmas I was tracing some of my LIVINGSTON family names in the census records, trying to verify and document information that I had found on my own ancestors. I finally found one particular LIVINGSTON ancestor in Monroe County, Indiana. I went to the census record and saw that he was a boarder in a house with a couple named WAMPLER. It had been awhile since I had done that search on my friend's family, but I knew that her father's family had a line of WAMPLERs.

I opened up her family file on my computer and sure enough, her WAMPLER family was from the same county in Indiana as my LIVINGSTON family. Through this discovery I was able to find even more of her family members and afterwards, wherever I found a LIVINGSTON family, I usually found a WAMPLER family living close by. What makes this so fascinating for us is that we met twenty-some years ago, and she has stayed with me and my family off and on for years. And now we have discovered that my ancestors were staying with her ancestors long before the two of us came along.

What are the chances that descendants of both families would meet and become best friends when we had no real connection to each other? It truly is a small world. And, just shows you never know what you will find when you start researching your family history.

RootsWeb

RootsWeb <www.rootsweb.com> is like a forest that has grown up without much pruning or thinning. It has been and continues to be created by a worldwide community of online and mostly amateur genealogists. It contains huge and tiny databases (including more than 465 million names in family trees), libraries, articles, how-to tips, personal websites (more than 30,000 independently authored websites containing about 9 million pages), archives, and all sorts of surprising treasures and tools tucked into its nooks and crannies. RootsWeb also provides numerous vehicles for the free exchange of information pertaining to family research—such as 30,000 mailing lists—and it sponsors many of the largest volunteer genealogy projects on the Web. Many genealogical and historical societies call RootsWeb home, as do various family associations, special-interest groups, and projects you might never have heard about. Most of the different areas of RootsWeb are built and maintained by dedicated volunteers who are avid, friendly genealogists often willing to go out of their way to help you.

Tracing your ancestors back through the past is mostly a do-it-yourself endeavor. However, RootsWeb contains tips and guides and links to information that will help you in your quest to discover your family's past. By making use of the incredible RootsWeb sources, you might find:

- Your family tree or part of it (but don't expect to find a complete one—or one that is 100 percent accurate).

- Historical and genealogical information about your ancestors, including extracts and abstracts of records such as censuses, wills, deeds, tax lists, local histories, family Bibles, old photographs, compiled works, and ship passenger lists.

- Websites dedicated to your surname (family name), a county your ancestors lived in, or research concerning a specific country.

- Cousins by the dozen via the mailing lists and message boards.

- Fellow researchers and friends who share your enthusiasm.

Now that you've learned a little about what you might find on RootsWeb, you should also know what you *won't* find; your experience with RootsWeb will be much more enjoyable if you start off with realistic goals and expectations of what information you can locate at RootsWeb. And keep in mind, RootsWeb does not have a staff to locate your ancestors or find relatives for you. Here are some examples of things you probably won't find:

- Your entire family tree, complete with photos, stories, and all relevant records.

- Information about living relatives, friends, and old loves (family history is about the past, not the present, although you probably will make connections with cousins and other relatives who will exchange information privately with you).

- Access to every record related to your family members.

- Someone who will "do" your genealogy for you and has the answer to all your questions.

Brand-New to Genealogy?

When most people get started on their genealogy, they want to know the best way to make progress in their research. Of course, it is fun to start searching immediately and try to find at least some of your family tree. However, the quickest and best way to make progress in your genealogical research is to learn how to research, study about the existing records that might answer your questions, and connect with a relative or someone who is further along or is more experienced than you are. Part of this hobby's fun is finding cousins you never knew existed and meeting helpful people who share your interest. Successful information gathering requires that you hone your research skills and learn not to expect instant answers to everything. The joy of genealogy is in the fun of the research, the thrill of the chase, putting the puzzle pieces together, and finding cousins around the world—not in how many names you can cram into your database.

Here are a few research tips and basic principles to help you get started:

- Always start with what you know and work backwards in time, generation to generation.

- Don't expect to find your ancestor's name spelled a certain way or even the same way twice. You will find your ancestors under many variant spellings of both the surname (family name) and the given name. Learning to *hear* how a name sounds with many accents can be most helpful. A spelling variation is NOT a name change. Your Michael Greene may turn into Mike Green, but he didn't change his name. Also, remember to look for your ancestor by his or her initials (G. W. Smith may be your George Washington) and by a nickname (your Martha Smith might have been called Patsy; your Robert Anderson may be recorded as Bob, Bobby, or Rob). More ancestors are overlooked in records due to spelling variants than any other reason. For more information, read a RootsWeb guide on spelling problems you might encounter at
<http://rwguide.rootsweb.com/lesson8.htm>.

- Remember to look for women by their married names and their maiden names (the names they were given at birth).

- If you can't locate any information about your ancestor, try searching for other members of the family who might be living in the same household (for example, the individual's parents, siblings, or in-laws). You just might find the person you were originally looking for.

- Databases go through updates and search features are enhanced—websites are dynamic and change regularly, so you may want to occasionally go back to certain sources to recheck for ancestors you missed the first time around.

- When searching for multiple individuals and multiple families over hundreds of years, it can be difficult to keep track of the details of all your searches. Consider keeping a research log of when you last searched a specific site, or for

a specific name. You'll save yourself much repeated effort. Also, keep track of all the sources you've visited when looking for information on a particular individual; this will keep you from duplicating work you've already done.

- Every time you learn a new fact, consider whether it is credible and accurate and whether it can be proved with additional sources. Relying on one piece of false information can set you down the wrong path and take your research off track for months and perhaps years.

- Don't forget to record where you find information. Document every fact you discover using complete and accurate references. You will find yourself coming back to these sources time and time again. And, if you end up sharing your research with others, you want them to be able to trace the path you followed.

- Don't give up! If at first you are unsuccessful, try again later when you have more information or a fresh eye.

Get Guidance

You can also take advantage of the free, interactive guides available at RootsWeb. *RootsWeb's Guide to Tracing Family Trees* was created by three professional genealogists who have diverse research backgrounds and expertise; the thirty-one guides within are designed to give you a central place to learn about a variety of topics related to genealogical research. Not just dull how-to instructions, they also contain links to websites and mailing lists that might be what you need to jump-start your family history project.

The guides are divided into three subject areas: general subjects, sources and record types, and countries and ethnic groups. The general subject guides such as "Where to Begin?" and "What's in a Name?" teach the fundamentals of research

and provide you with a foundation on the records you need
to compile your family tree. In the sources and record type
guides, you'll find lessons on various types of records and
documents (e.g., tax records, census records, church records,
military records, and ship passenger records); this section
also contains guides on such topics as fraternal organizations,
newspapers and directories, and genealogy software. Finally,
the third group of guides teaches you how to look for your
ancestors based on location such as Canada, South Africa,
Germany, Wales, and more. It also gives information on a
variety of ethnic groups—African American, Native American,
Jewish, among others.

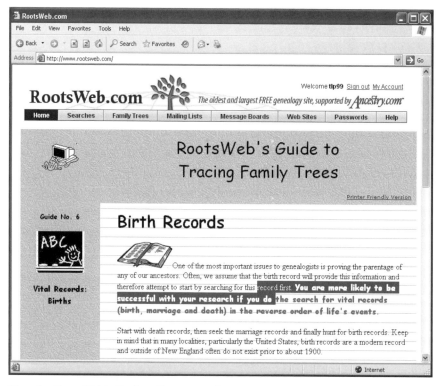

The online RootsWeb's Guide to Tracing Family Trees

These guides can all be accessed from the homepage. Find the "Getting Started" section and click the "RootsWeb's Guide To Tracing Family Trees" link or go to <http://rwguide.rootsweb. com>.

Brand-New to RootsWeb?

Hunting for your ancestors can yield a great deal of information—some of which you may find important and interesting and some of which you may not. Before you jump right in to searching, think about what it is you wish to learn on RootsWeb. Not everything is packaged neatly under a specific database. If you want to find your grandparents' marriage record, searching for surname websites is probably not the most effective way to go about it. Think about topics where the information you want might be found. You might want to explore:

- **Surnames.** Many of your searches at RootsWeb (and elsewhere) will be by surnames. You can learn more about your ethnicity, variations of your name to use in searches, migration and immigration patterns, and perhaps even discover a few distant relatives.

- **Localities.** Learning the local history of places your ancestors lived in can help you better understand them and what challenges they faced in life. Focus on the places where they once lived, particularly as young and middle-age adults; this is the time of life when they likely created records you might find. Additionally, you might discover information about your ancestor in his or her in-laws' or neighbors' records.

- **Family Trees.** If you want to get a jump start on your research and see what others have learned about your family or you want to verify information you already have, family trees are the place to go. RootsWeb has many family trees—millions of them can be found in WorldConnect *and* on private websites.

- **Documents.** Records are often the most sought after items in family history. RootsWeb hosts millions of Web pages where you might find such things as scans of marriage and census records, or transcriptions (word-for-word copies of records, including errors and misspellings) of wills and court records.

- **Living Persons.** If you seek living relatives, the best way to make connections is by posting on the message boards (by surname or locality) and utilizing the mailing lists.

- **How-to Information.** In addition to *RootsWeb's Guide To Tracing Family Trees,* you can learn more about researching and find a great deal of help through the various mailing lists, message boards, and websites hosted by RootsWeb— both personal sites and those of various historical and genealogical societies and others.

Focus Your Research

Once you've decided on the area you want to focus on, you can try out a couple of RootsWeb's "research templates." RootsWeb has created pages that group together great lists of resources to get you started. Do you have a surname you are interested in researching? Go to the homepage and find the "Research Templates" section, then click the "Surnames" link or go to <http://resources.rootsweb.com/surnames>. When you click on a surname, you'll find links to relevant mailing lists, personal Web pages, and search templates—all on one page. Are you searching for information about ancestors in a specific location in America? Go to the homepage and find the "Research Templates" section, then click the "United States"

The "research template" for Washington County, Kansas

link or go to <http://resources.rootsweb.com/USA>. You can narrow your search to specific counties where you might find links to local genealogical societies, online records, and, of course, mailing lists.

Navigating Around the Site

RootsWeb can be somewhat of a challenge to navigate. To get the most out of the website, be adventurous and explore, but understand that there is no master search engine that will enable you to find all possible references to your ancestor— somewhere on RootsWeb—just by typing in a surname. You will have to do the digging, but that's the joy of the search.

Use these links to log in to your account or access your member information.

The RootsWeb navigation bar remains at the top of most RootsWeb pages regardless of where you are in the site. Use the bar to quickly navigate to the homepage or to access other major features.

Each major feature has a heading with links to related databases and tools.

Click a blue link to access a specific feature, database, or tool.

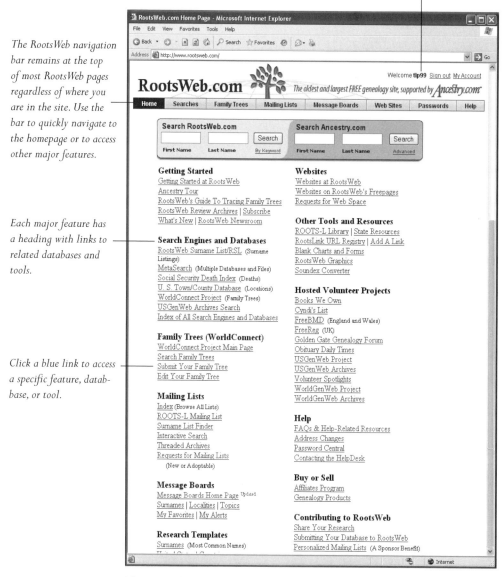

The RootsWeb homepage

Homepage Overview

When you first access the RootsWeb homepage <www.rootsweb. com>, you might find it a bit intimidating because of the many headings and links. At first glance, it may seem like a lot of information to wade through, but with this guide, you'll be familiar with all of RootsWeb's great features in no time. At the top of the homepage you'll notice a bar of navigational buttons: Home, Searches, Family Trees, Mailing Lists, Message Boards, Web Sites, Passwords, and Help. The Home button takes you to the homepage, the face of RootsWeb; the Searches button gives you access to the search engines that are used most often and also the user-contributed databases; the Family Trees button takes you to the "homepage" for the WorldConnect trees, a large database of user-submitted family trees; the Mailing Lists and Message Boards buttons take you to their homepages; the Web Sites button gives you access to websites that are either hosted by RootsWeb or just linked to it; the Passwords and Help buttons link you to help for the site. Regardless of where you are on RootsWeb, these buttons remain at the top of each page, so you can easily navigate to any of these major areas of the site. The headings and sections on the homepage can also direct you.

Searching RootsWeb

You'll find that most searches you do on RootsWeb are done within a specific database or feature. Each search engine works a little bit differently, and you may get different results, depending on how you use them. To utilize RootsWeb to its fullest and for successful genealogical research, investigate and utilize each one of these search engines. This section explains two ways in which you can search RootsWeb in general. In subsequent chapters, you'll learn how to search specific databases such as the message boards and family trees.

Search Thingy

Search Thingy (found on the Searches tab) is a rather silly name for an older, site-wide search engine for various Web pages housed at RootsWeb. Unfortunately, the search engine hasn't been updated regularly, so the results you'll get won't include information that has been entered recently. If you do want to try out Search Thingy, try searching for keywords in addition to the usual name searches—localities where your ancestors resided, or a topic of interest, such as passenger lists, epidemics, or outlaws.

Another option you can use to get similar but better results is to utilize the popular Google search engine <www. google.com>. You can find information that might be buried at RootsWeb by entering an ancestor's name, locality or subject, and the term "rootsweb":

given name surname +rootsweb

surname +locality +rootsweb

surname +keyword +rootsweb

And because Web pages and various databases are fluid— constantly being changed, added to, or taken down—periodic searches should be conducted for best results.

Meta Search fields

Meta Search

The Meta Search is available from the Searches tab and also from the homepage under the "Search Engines and Databases" section. This search engine lets you search multiple databases from one central location, including WorldConnect, the SSDI, the RootsWeb Surname List (RSL), vital records, and other databases containing information from sources like newspapers and obituaries.

Keep in mind, you can only search by surname, given name, or keyword.

General Search Tips

As you start searching through databases, keep some of these general search tips in mind:

- **Given Names.** Try alternate spellings and abbreviations for your ancestor's given name(s). Sometimes only an initial or abbreviation is used, such as Chas. for Charles, Thos. for Thomas, and Wm. for William. Also look for variations and different spellings—Eliza, Beth, Liz, or Liza, for Elizabeth; Alex for Alexander; Jim for James; Jon for John.

- **Surnames (family names).** Many of your searches at RootsWeb (and elsewhere) will be by surnames, but make sure you search for spelling variations for all names. You may find your great-grandpa John Kelly listed as Kelley, Killey, Kelle, or O'Kelly. Just because the name is not spelled exactly as you have come to know or use it, does not mean there was a name change or that the Kelly and Kelle families are not related. Most of our surnames have undergone some spelling changes through the centuries. If you are looking for an immigrant ancestor, look for his or her name as it would be in his or her native language.

- **Soundex.** Some of the databases at RootsWeb let you use Soundex searches. Soundex allows you to search for last names that "sound like" the one you're looking for. This can be useful because record keepers may have made spelling errors, or created "Americanized" versions of foreign names. Try out Soundex even if you think the spelling is obvious. Remember, even Smith can be "misspelled" (e.g., Smithe, Smyth, Smythe).

- **Date Ranges.** If you are searching for an ancestor who has a common name, a great way to narrow your search is to use date ranges. You'll get fewer search results and find it much easier to uncover that ancestor. Be careful though, some databases only match search results exactly. If you include too much information, you may miss the individual you're looking for. You might try only specifying a month and a year instead of the full date.

- **Wildcards.** Wildcards (such as the asterisk "*" and the question mark "?") are used in searches to replace a certain number of characters in a search term. Use the asterisk wildcard to view all words that begin with the same stem— up to six characters. For example, a search for "fran*" will return matches such as Fran, Franny, Frank, Frannie, and Frankie. Use a question mark for a single character. For example, a search for "Hans?n" will return matches such as Hansen and Hanson.

Ready to start digging up your past? Let's start by exploring how you can do this using the WorldConnect family trees at RootsWeb.

Meeting at Old Burial Grounds

By Susan Kundert,
RootsWeb User

After I posted an update to my RootsWeb family tree, I received numerous queries from other researchers. One query in particular led to a series of encounters with heretofore unknown, but closely-related cousins that is nothing short of phenomenal.

I received a message from a cousin in Coldwater, Michigan, who is a descendant, as I am, of American Revolutionary War veteran Gorg Daniel CONRAD (born 1734). Through an exchange of e-mails, we determined that this cousin's great-grandfather, George CONRAD, was the brother of Mary E. CONRAD, first wife of my own great-grandfather, Joseph Kesler BALTHASER. We decided we would meet, and I would guide my cousin and her husband to the family burial grounds in Clear Creek Township.

Before heading to the Conrad Cemetery, we poured over old atlases and local history books at the Fairfield County Library. On one of the pages, we noticed an engraving of an elegant 1870s mansion that had originally belonged to a cousin, William CONRAD. I knew the mansion was on the way to the cemetery, so we stopped to take a photo of this lovingly restored part of our family heritage and then headed down the road to the burial ground.

A few minutes later, a new, shiny pickup truck pulled up. The driver asked if we were CONRAD descendants. He said he was a descendant as well, although his surname was SHUPE. From my research, I knew that anyone with the SHUPE surname in this area was almost certainly a descendant of my third great-grandparents, John SHUPE and Elizabeth CONRAD. I was flabbergasted to learn that this stranger by the side of the road was a direct descendant of not only my SHUPE/CONRAD line, but of all but one of my other maternal direct lines as well.

As we celebrated our newfound relationships, our Fairfield County cousin suggested we continue our discussion at his home, which turned out to be that elegant, lovingly restored mansion we had stopped to photograph on our way to the cemetery.

WorldConnect Family Trees

With more than 465 million names on file, WorldConnect is one of the largest collections of free family trees available online. Submitted by family historians from around the world, these trees can literally save you years of research and enable you to discover cousins on many branches of your family tree. Not only do they provide you with valuable information, they are also a way to contact others who may be researching your relatives. New researchers often think of only their immediate family when they begin to search, but there may be dozens of cousins out there who descend from the same ancestors as you or who connect to your tree via another branch. Even in-laws, half-, and step-relatives may have valuable information.

Online trees are also a great way for you to share and exchange the family information you have gathered. By submitting your tree to WorldConnect, you may help someone complete their family picture or find a distant cousin to collaborate with.

History of WorldConnect

WorldConnect has a genealogy of its own. In its early days in 1994 and 1995, very few genealogical databases were online, and there were only a few genealogy-related websites. A group of people formed the GenWeb group to discuss the possibilities of combining family history and the Internet. During the next few years, computer programmers experimented with converting GEDCOMs to formats that could be read online. Then on 10 November 1999, RootsWeb announced the launch of the WorldConnect Project after staff members and users submitted 5.5 million records during a four-week testing period. Now, WorldConnect grows daily as more and more family historians share their information.

Searching for Family Trees

WorldConnect has several types of search tools you can use to quickly access the family trees that most interest you. If you're just beginning your family search or you know the exact database you want to access, you might want to use the basic search options; if you're a more skilled researcher, try the global search.

Basic Search

To begin a basic search, click the **Family Trees** tab. A group of four different basic search options will appear on the left side of the page:

- **Surname and given name.** You can enter an individual's name to view every family tree that contains this person.

- **Specific database.** You can jump to a specific database by entering its user code.

Note: Each family tree is identified by a unique
user code. To find a user code for a family
tree *someone else* submitted, search for their
WorldConnect file. The user code appears at the
end of the Web address after the equal sign. For
example, "winch" is the user code in this Web
address: **http://worldconnect.rootsweb.com/cgi-bin/igm.
cgi?db=winch**

- **Database by keyword(s).** You can search for
keywords that appear in the family tree, e-mail
address, submitter name, and even the titles,
headers, and footers of the trees. This option
is especially helpful for researching common
surnames. If you are looking for a "Smith" who
married a "Snickerdoodle," you can increase your
chances of locating a tree with their information
by entering both surnames in this field rather
than only one surname in the "Surname and given
name" field.

- **Database by surname(s).** You can search
for databases that contain certain surnames.
Enter a space or a comma between each
surname. The search results will show you the
number of people in the tree with your specified
surname(s).

**Search Family Trees
at WorldConnect**

Advanced Search

More than **460 million** names on file

Surname

Given
Name

GO

or -- jump to a specific database

Database

GO

or -- find a database by keyword(s)

GO

or -- find a database by surname(s)

GO

Basic search options

Global Search
The global search can be used for both basic searches
and detailed, advanced searches. You must enter information in
at least one field, but you complete as many additional fields as
you would like.

To begin a global search, click the **Family Trees** tab, then click the "Advanced Search" link at the top of the page or on the homepage, find the "Family Trees (WorldConnect)" section, and click the "Search Family Trees" link.

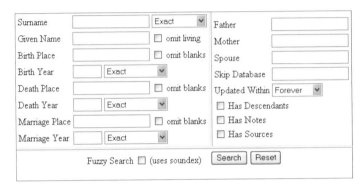

Global search options

Complete any of these fields as necessary:

In this field	Do this
Surname	Enter a surname (last name or family name). Make sure to try different spellings, including spacing variations (van Horn and vanhorn, or O'Brien and OBrien).
	From the drop-down list, choose whether the search is for exact matches (surnames with the same spelling), Soundex matches (surnames with the same Soundex code), or Metaphone matches (surnames that have a similar English pronunciation).
Given name	Enter a given name (first name). If you enter a first *and* middle name, matches will include both names—but not necessarily in that order. For example, a search for Mary Jane will result in matches for "Mary Jane" and "Jane Mary."
	If you are not looking for a specific person or if want to broaden your search, leave this field blank.

In this field	Do this
Birth Place, Death Place, or Marriage Place	Enter a location (a town, township, county, state, country, or province).
	For U.S. localities enter either a state's name (e.g., Tennessee) or a two-letter abbreviation (e.g., TN) and you will get the same matches. If you are entering a country, try searching by its name and by its standard abbreviation.
Birth Year, Death Year, or Marriage Year	Enter the year of the life event.
	From the drop-down list, choose whether the search is for exact matches (the year you entered) or a date range (plus or minus the year you entered).
Omit Blanks	Click this checkbox to remove any matches where this field in a family tree is blank or empty.
Father, Mother, or Spouse	Enter a surname, given name, or both.
Skip Database	The Skip Database feature lets you "ignore" certain family trees. This is especially convenient if you don't want to see your submitted files in your search results.
	Enter a database's user code. To ignore several databases, put a space between each user code. For example, enter "jsmith adamsg smithreed smithtx." Do not use commas or enter URLs (Web addresses) in this field.
	Note: Each family tree is identified by a unique user code. To find a user code for a family tree *someone else* submitted, search for their WorldConnect file. The user code appears at the end of the Web address after the equal sign. For example, "winch" is the user code in this Web address: http://worldconnect.rootsweb.com/cgi-bin/igm.cgi?db=winch
	To find a user code for a family tree *you* submitted, click the **Passwords** tab and request your WorldConnect user code and password. You will receive an e-mail of all your user codes and passwords.

In this field	Do this
Updated Within	Choose an option from the drop-down list to restrict your search to files that have been submitted, modified, or updated within a certain period of time. Choose "Forever" to search through all available databases.
Has Descendants	Click the checkbox to find only files that contain the individual you're searching for *and* their descendants.
Has Notes	Click the checkbox to find only files that have user notes.
Has Sources	Click the checkbox to find only files that have sources.
Fuzzy Search	Short for "fuzzy logic," this geek term means that the search will return *probable* matches along with *exact* matches. Click the checkbox to search all name (except surname) and location fields using Soundex matching.

Tips for Successful Searches

If your searches haven't turned up the results you were hoping for, try some of these search tips:

- If you're using the global search, try entering information in fewer fields. This will broaden your search and return more matches.

- Use wildcards in name fields—wildcards let you view all names that begin with the same letters. Enter at least the first three letters of the name, followed by an asterisk. For example, a search for "Har*" will return matches such as Harold, Harry and Harriett, while "Peter*" will give you results such as Peter, Peters, Peterson, Petersen, and Peterman.

- Use the Soundex option for surnames. Names are often misspelled in historical records or even indexed incorrectly. Soundex lets you search for last names that "sound like" the one you're looking for. This option is useful because even names like Smith can be "misspelled" as Smithe, Smyth, and Smythe.

- Try variant spellings of names, nicknames, and initials— each submitter has control over his or her tree, so spelling variations are quite common.

- Be sure to search for women under their maiden names.

- For location fields, search for misspellings and abbreviations. For example, if the location is Tennessee, you might search for "Tenessee," "TN," and "Tns." If the name includes a space, such as "San Francisco," do searches both with and without the space. For locations like St. Louis, try searching with both "St." and "Saint."

Understanding Your Search Results

Depending on the type of search you perform, you may

- Go directly to a specific database. The search takes you to the tree's "homepage." At the top of the page, you will see the tree's title and owner and the last time the database was updated.

- See a list of databases. After each database name, you'll find the name and e-mail of the tree's owner and additional information about the tree such as its title. Click the database link to access the tree's "homepage."

- See a list of names that match your search criteria. At the top of the search results, you can see the number of matches as well as which of those matches you are currently viewing.

The columns for each match provide you with the following information:

Column	Information Found in Column
Name	This column lists all records that match the search criteria you entered. If you entered "John Smith," the results will include all records where "John" is either the given or middle name and "Smith" is the surname. In addition to every tree that contains John Smith, the results will also include trees with names such as Aaron John Smith, Zebulon John Smith, and everything in between. Click a name link to access that individual's record within his or her family tree. From this page, you can navigate to other individuals within the tree as well. To access the tree's "homepage," click the "Index" link at the top of the page.
Birth/Christening Date and Place	This column shows birth dates and places (if they are in the individual's record). Christening dates and places (labeled as such) will automatically be listed as an alternative if the birth date and place are not in the file.
Death/Burial Date and Place	This column shows death and burial dates and places (if they are in the individual's record).
Database	This column shows the database's user code (the unique name chosen by the submitter for the specific family tree). Click a database link to access the "homepage" of the family tree.

> Note: The Order record? and Other Matches fields link you to third-party sites such as Ancestry.com, which may have information for that individual in other records on their sites. RootsWeb is not responsible for the content on these third-party sites.

Beneath the individual's name, you may see several icons:

 The magnifying glass icon appears when there are matches for this individual in Ancestry.com databases.

Click the icon to go to an Ancestry.com search results page—matches are for both free and subscription databases.

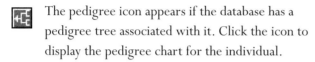 The pedigree icon appears if the database has a pedigree tree associated with it. Click the icon to display the pedigree chart for the individual.

The descendants icon indicates that the individual has children listed in the family tree. Click the icon to view a descendant outline that starts with the individual.

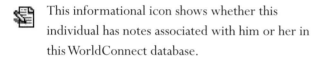 This informational icon shows whether this individual has notes associated with him or her in this WorldConnect database.

This informational icon shows whether source information is included with the individual's data.

Beneath the birth and death dates and places, you might also see the names of the individual's father, mother, or spouse. Click these links to go to the individual record for the father, mother, or spouse.

Viewing a Family Tree

The "homepage" of any family tree database in WorldConnect gives you basic information about the file: the submitter's name and e-mail address, the number of records in the family tree, and the date it was last updated. This information can be found at the top of every page in the tree. In addition, you may find links to the submitter's personal websites or comments they have left pertaining to their files.

You can access an individual's record in the tree by entering a surname or full name in the search box or click the link for a letter in the alphabet to browse for individuals in the tree whose surname begins with that letter. Once you have located a person you are interested in, you can click on his or her name to view the individual's record.

The Individual Record

An individual record displays all the information in a given family tree for one person (e.g., their name, gender, ID number, parents, spouses, and children). Notes and sources will be shown, if available. You may see blue links for parents, spouses, or children; click these links to view the individual records for each of these individuals.

At the top of the individual's record, you'll notice a group of links. These links help you navigate to other sections of the family tree, take you to a variety of reports and charts, and may even let you download the tree or add Post-em notes. The options that appear vary for each person in the family tree and not every selection is available in every family tree; the options

---

Index | Descendancy | Register | Pedigree | Ahnentafel | Add Post-em

- *ID:* I34605
- *Name:* James Clarence Bobbitt
- *Sex:* M
- *Birth:* 28 JUL 1858 in Varna,Marshall,Il
- *Reference Number:* H1169743

Father: John William Bobbitt b: 9 JUN 1831 in Cerulean Springs,Trigg,Ky
Mother: Julia M. Hoyt b: 6 SEP 1834 in Chillicothe,Ross,Oh

Marriage 1 Margaret Rebecca Shanklin b: 12 JUL 1863 in Lacon,Marshall,Il

- *Married:* ABT 1883 in Peoria,Peoria,Il

Children

1. Charity Maydette Bobbitt b: 10 MAR 1883 in Stella,Richardson,Ne
2. James Leslie Bobbitt b: 19 SEP 1884 in Stella,Richardson,Ne
3. Mary Eleanor Bobbitt b: 10 APR 1886 in Beatrice,Richardson,Ne
4. Bessie Anita Bobbitt b: 14 DEC 1888 in Carrier,Garfield,Ok
5. Alta Maud Bobbitt b: 9 FEB 1892 in Anthony,Harper,Ks
6. Veda Myrtle Bobbitt b: 29 OCT 1894 in Cleo Springs,Woods,It
7. Bobbitt b: ABT 1896 in Cleo Springs,Woods,It
8. Living Bobbitt
9. Living Bobbitt
10. Living Bobbitt

Individual record

that appear depend on the information in the actual file *and* the preferences of the tree's owner.

The Index

The Index link shows the names of all individuals in a family tree, beginning with the specified individual. If the index contains multiple pages, you can click the "Previous Page" and "Next Page" links at the bottom of the page to navigate through the index. You can also click any of the individual links to go to another person's individual record or use the search box to find a specific individual.

Enter **surname** OR **surname**, **given** to find:
[BOBBITT, JAMES CLAR] [List] Advanced Search

No Surname < A B C D E F G H I J K L M N O P Q R S T U V W X Y Z >

BOBBITT, JAMES CLARENCE b: 28 Jul 1858 in VARNA, MARSHALL, IL
BOBBITT, JAMES LESLIE b: 19 Sep 1884 in STELLA, RICHARDSON, NE
BOBBITT, JESSIE JULIA b: 3 Mar 1872 in PEORIA, PEORIA, IL
BOBBITT, JOHN SEYMORE b: 7 Nov 1853 in PEORIA, PEORIA, IL
BOBBITT, JOHN WILLIAM b: 9 Jun 1831 in CERULEAN SPRINGS, TRIGG, KY d: 24 Aug 1909 in DAWSON, RICHARDSON, NE
BOBBITT, Living
BOBBITT, Living
BOBBITT, Living
BOBBITT, Living
BOBBITT, MALISSA b: abt 1827 in CERULEAN SPRINGS, TRIGG, KY
BOBBITT, MARY ELEANOR b: 10 Apr 1886 in BEATRICE, RICHARDSON, NE
BOBBITT, SARA ELINOR b: 14 Nov 1863 in VARNA, MARSHALL, IL
BOBBITT, SARAH ELEANOR b: 1879
BOBBITT, TERESA b: abt 1825 in CERULEAN SPRINGS, TRIGG, KY

Index of individuals in the family tree

Descendancy Report

The Descendancy link displays a report that shows you an individual's descendants including birth and death dates, with a maximum of ten generations.

You can return to the individual's record by clicking the "Individual" link at the top of any report.

```
1 MARGARET REBECCA SHANKLIN b: 12 Jul 1863
 + JAMES CLARENCE BOBBITT b: 28 Jul 1858
   2  BOBBITT b: abt 1896
   2 Living BOBBITT
   2 ALTA MAUD BOBBITT b: 9 Feb 1892
    + NOAH ALONZO FORD b: abt 1890
   2 BESSIE ANITA BOBBITT b: 14 Dec 1888
    + FRED DOUGLAS SHEPARD b: abt 1886
   2 CHARITY MAYDETTE BOBBITT b: 10 Mar 1883
    + BURDETTE CROSSMAN b: abt 1883
   2 CLYDE SYLVIUS BOBBITT b: 2 Sep 1901
   2 JAMES LESLIE BOBBITT b: 19 Sep 1884
   2 Living BOBBITT
   2 MARY ELEANOR BOBBITT b: 10 Apr 1886
    + ELMER PARSONS b: abt 1884
   2 Living BOBBITT
    + HAROLD ARTHUR REED b: 2 Aug 1895
   2 VEDA MYRTLE BOBBITT b: 29 Oct 1894
```

Descendancy report

Register Report

The Register link displays a narrative report that shows you an individual's descendants including names, dates, and places, with a maximum of six generations.

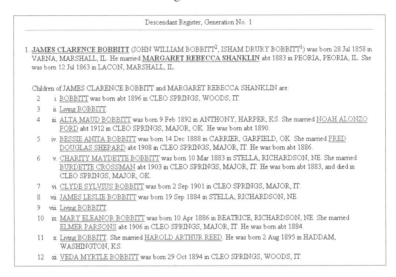

Register report

Pedigree Chart

The Pedigree link displays a pedigree chart, the traditional chart used to show an individual and his or her ancestors. WorldConnect offers two formats for pedigree charts. The "table format" is the traditional, graphical chart with branching lines, and it displays a maximum of four generations. The table format

Text-only pedigree chart

appears by default. A compact text-only format is also available and displays a maximum of ten generations. To view the text-only pedigree, click the "Display pedigree in text format" link.

Ahnentafel

Ahnentafel is a German word meaning "ancestor table." The Ahnentafel begins with an individual and moves backward to his or her ancestors—it also shows two family lines in the same report. You can view up to six generations of an individual's ancestors on one page of an Ahnentafel chart. Click the "Ahnentafel link" to access this chart.

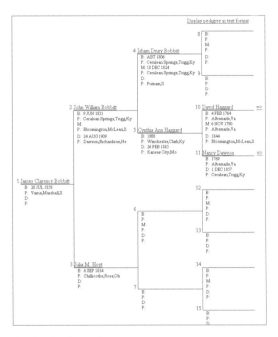

Graphical pedigree chart

Ahnentafel, Generation No. 1

1. JAMES CLARENCE BOBBITT was born 28 Jul 1858 in VARNA, MARSHALL, IL. He was the son of **2. JOHN WILLIAM BOBBITT** and **3. JULIA M. HOYT**. He married MARGARET REBECCA SHANKLIN abt 1883 in PEORIA, PEORIA, IL. She was born 12 Jul 1863 in LACON, MARSHALL, IL.

Ahnentafel, Generation No. 2

2. JOHN WILLIAM BOBBITT was born 9 Jun 1831 in CERULEAN SPRINGS, TRIGG, KY, and died 24 Aug 1909 in DAWSON, RICHARDSON, NE. He was the son of **4. ISHAM DRURY BOBBITT** and **5. CYNTHIA Ann Haggard**

3. JULIA M. HOYT was born 6 Sep 1834 in CHILLICOTHE, ROSS, OH.

   Children of JULIA M. HOYT and JOHN WILLIAM BOBBITT are:
   i. ALLEN EUGENE BOBBITT was born 27 Jan 1877 in PEORIA, PEORIA, IL. He married ELLA abt 1899. She was born abt 1879.
   ii. CORNELIA OLIVE BOBBITT was born 8 Mar 1856 in PEORIA, PEORIA, IL. She married SHIER abt 1877 in DAWSON, NE. He was born abt 1855 in DAWSON, NE.
   iii. FRANCIS MARION BOBBITT was born 9 Jul 1868 in PEORIA, PEORIA, IL. He married JULIA LUCY COMSTOCK abt 1890. She was born abt 1870.
   1. iv. JAMES CLARENCE BOBBITT was born 28 Jul 1858 in VARNA, MARSHALL, IL. He married MARGARET REBECCA SHANKLIN abt 1883 in PEORIA, PEORIA, IL. She was born 12 Jul 1863 in LACON, MARSHALL, IL.

Ahnentafel

> Note: If you want to print a chart or report without banner ads or any of superfluous material, click the "Printer Friendly Version" link at the bottom of the page. Click the "Return to normal view" link at the top of the page to return to the report.

Things to Keep in Mind

As you look through the trees on WorldConnect, keep in mind that it is not one huge master database but rather is a collection of individual family trees. Each file remains separate and is not merged into a giant database because each file belongs to the person who submitted it. The files are the work of many thousands of individuals independently researching their family histories.

As a result, you will find some duplication. When doing a search, use as many of the advanced search features as possible to help eliminate same-name individuals who are not actually the individual you wish to locate. If you have done that and still find duplication, it might mean that multiple submitters have the individual you are looking for in their files. That can be good news because it means that any or all of them might have discovered information you do not have.

However, remember that RootsWeb does not have a staff that checks, verifies, or judges the accuracy of the trees found at WorldConnect. This information is provided by individual submitters. Evaluation of the accuracy of the information is left up to you. Information found at WorldConnect, like any genealogical material acquired from Internet sources, books, or via hundreds of other ways, only provides clues and contacts for your further research—not proof of a pedigree or a family history.

Downloading a Family Tree

Anyone who adds a tree to WorldConnect can decide whether or not other users can download their family tree file. If this option is available, you will see a "Download GEDCOM" link at the top of any tree page. (If the tree you want isn't available for download, you might want to send an e-mail to the tree's owner—they might be happy to share with you on a more private basis.)

> Note: The file you download will begin with the individual whose page you are viewing. If you want the file to start with a different individual, choose the "Download GEDCOM" link from *their* tree page. The number of generations you can download varies depending on the size of the file and the number of generations the submitter will allow you to access.

To download a tree, click the "Download GEDCOM" link at the top or bottom of the family tree page. You can choose whether the file contains the ancestors or descendants of the selected individual, the number of generations in the file (the maximum is ten), and more.

Adding a Post-em Note

Post-em notes are the electronic equivalent of a sticky note and let you add your "two cents" to trees you find. For example, if you find a discrepancy in your ancestor's birth date in another individual's tree, you can create a Post-em note that attaches to your ancestor in their database. You can include the date you think is accurate, your e-mail address, a link to another website, or anything you think would be useful. If a note has been added to a tree database, you will see a "View

Post-em" link towards the bottom of the page. Click the link to access the note.

Post-em notes can also be a useful tool for your own trees you've added to WorldConnect. Because you cannot "edit" your family tree once it is in WorldConnect (you must submit an updated file), Post-em notes help you add corrections or additions or fill in missing pieces of your tree until you have a chance to update it.

To add a Post-em note, click the "Add Post-em" link at the top of any family tree page. For more information, click the **Help** tab and find the "Post-em Notes" section.

Tana Lord	tlord@myfamilyinc.com	2007-02-23 16:46:06
Other records contain conflicting information about the date of death--cemetery records record the date as 17 December 1972.		

Post-em note

Contacting the Owner of a Tree

At the top of every tree page you will see the tree owner's name and e-mail address. The Contact field shows the owner's name. Next to this you will see the owner's e-mail address in a speckled gray graphic. This graphic has no special meaning—it simply helps protect e-mail addresses from unethical websites that try to steal e-mail addresses from other sites. If you find that the e-mail address is hard to read, you can click the Refresh button on your browser to reload the Web page.

Contact: Tana Lord tlord@myfamilyinc.com

E-mail address display on RootsWeb

Submitting Your Own Family Tree

By submitting your own family tree, you may help others extend the branches of their family tree. And you may find

some great people to collaborate with. You will always retain ownership of your tree, which means you are free to update it or remove it whenever you want. And you can submit as many family trees as you would like.

Before You Begin

Take a few minutes now to prepare your file in your genealogy program; this can save you from having to make changes later on. Make sure the file is as accurate as possible—check for misspellings, dates that don't make sense, anything that could send another researcher down the wrong path. You might want to remove or edit any information that appears for living individuals to protect their privacy (you can also hide this information during the setup process).

Now, you will need to create a GEDCOM (.ged) file of the family tree. If you have any questions on how to do this, check the user's manual for your genealogy program, or go to <http:// helpdesk.rootsweb.com/FAQ/wcgedcom3.html> for instructions.

Submit the Tree

To submit the tree to WorldConnect, click the **Family Trees** tab, then click the "Start Here" link at the top of the page or on the homepage, find the "Family Trees (WorldConnect)" section, and click the "Submit Your Family Tree" link.

> Note: If you don't feel comfortable uploading a tree yourself and would still like your family tree to appear in WorldConnect, you can submit your file through the mail and a RootsWeb staff member will upload the tree for you. For more information, click the Family Trees tab. Then find the "FAQs and HELP" section, and click the "How to submit files via the mail" link.

GEDCOM

GEDCOM is an acronym for **GE**nealogical **D**ata **COM**munications. It is a file format developed by the Family History Department of The Church of Jesus Christ of Latter-day Saints (LDS). It provides a flexible and uniform format for exchanging computerized genealogical data and allows you to share files with other researchers who may not use the same genealogy program (e.g., *Family Tree Maker*, PAF, etc.) that you do.

User Codes and Passwords

The first step in uploading your file is to create a unique user code and password for your family tree file. User codes help you keep track of your files and also identify the file so that others can search for it. Enter a user code that has three to sixteen characters (letters, numbers, a hyphen, or underscore characters only); it *cannot* contain any spaces. Then, enter a password. You may want to write these down—in case you ever forget them.

Setup Options

You can now choose the standard or advanced setup. The standard setup gives you the opportunity to change a few display options (e.g., your page headers and footers) and determine whether other members can download your family tree. The first time you submit a tree, it is recommended that you choose the standard setup. The advanced setup gives you all the options of the standard setup with some added customizations; you can choose the number of generations that appear in reports and charts, and you have more flexibility in determine what information appears for "living" individuals in your tree.

On the page that appears, enter your name and e-mail address, then click the **Setup** button. You're ready to set up your file. Change any necessary setup options, and click the **Upload/Update** button.

That's it. You've just helped the community grow—and maybe you're even on your way to finding a long-lost cousin! And remember, this is *your* family tree; you can update it or even remove the file at any time.

Finding a Lost Father

By Mary Beth Rausch ,
RootsWeb User

I began researching for my father-in-law a couple of years ago. I checked every website and board I could find, but I wasn't successful in finding information on his father, who disappeared in 1925.

My father-in-law's parents divorced and Jim [my father-in-law] and his brother never found out what happened to their dad. Their mom didn't want to talk about him. Jim felt sad about never seeing his dad again and would think about him time after time throughout his life. I really wanted to find out something for him.

One day, I posted information about his dad on a RootsWeb message board. Later, I received an e-mail from someone who was researching the same name. He suggested I get in touch with another woman, so I e-mailed her, and found out that my father-in-law's dad had remarried and moved to another state. He and his wife had eleven children.

My father-in-law had eleven siblings he didn't know about! My contact got in touch with one of the siblings, and at first there was disbelief because most of them had never heard of another family. The older ones had heard rumors but didn't believe them. I sent copies of his Aiken County, Minnesota, birth certificate and his sister's death certificate and a couple of pictures of Jim for her to share with them. That clinched it—Jim is definitely his father's son. They were overcome by how much he looked like their father.

They wanted to meet Jim. I called him and told him that I had found out where his father went and about his family. Jim was very touched and both happy and sad. Sad that his father had passed away before he could see him again but so happy to have all those siblings. Soon a trip was planned for him to go to Washington State to meet with his new family. Jim was overcome with happiness as he met about fifty new relatives. What a treasure both of the past, and a future of getting acquainted with family.

Getting the Most out of Message Boards

Message boards are an excellent way to find someone to help you with your research by sharing information or expertise. Millions of users post messages asking for specific information, offering advice, or providing that missing clue to a fellow user. Post a message in the appropriate forum, and it will be available to the millions who utilize message boards. Since message boards are universally searchable, they make an excellent place for you to post a query about your brick-wall ancestors, to archive data and photos, and to search for others who might be looking for your ancestors.

Currently RootsWeb has more than 160,000 message boards; they are divided into three main categories: surnames, localities, and genealogical research topics. Surnames are broken down alphabetically; localities are separated by continents, then countries, and subsequently to states, counties, and their equivalents; research topics include everything from adoptions and folklore to DNA and newspaper research.

{ Note: The message boards on Ancestry.com and RootsWeb.com have been combined. When you read or post a message on the RootsWeb message boards, the same message will appear on the Ancestry.com message boards.

Use this search to find specific names or keywords in any message in any board.

Use this search to find a specific message board. Click letters in the alphabet to view a list of surnames.

Click the folder links to find message boards by geographic location or topic.

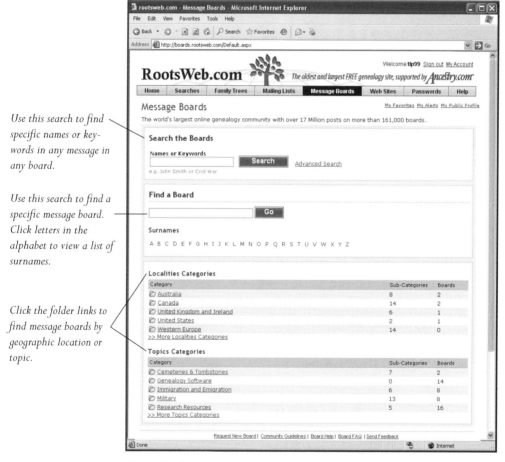

Message boards homepage

Searching the Boards

The message boards have several types of searches you can use to narrow in on that elusive ancestor or favorite research topic, whether you just want to take a look around or do some in-depth searching.

Quick Searches

To familiarize yourself with the message boards, you might want to try a couple simple searches. Click the **Message Boards** tab at the top of any RootsWeb page (or go to <http://boards.rootsweb.com>). To search *every* message board for a particular keyword, phrase, or name, enter the term in the **Search the Boards** field. For example, if you enter the surname "Hewitt," your search results will show every message in which the Hewitt name is used, regardless of which board the post is attached to. To search for a specific message board, such as for a surname, enter the keyword or name in the **Find a Board** field. For example, enter the surname "Hewitt" in this field. Your search results will show boards that specifically focus on this surname or similar keywords.

{ Note: As you type in a term, you'll notice that a drop-down list shows you similar terms you can choose from.

When searching for a specific board, a drop-down list will show similar terms.

Browse the Boards

Another way to find a message board of interest is to browse the entire collection. You can navigate through the boards by clicking categories and then sub-categories. To browse the surname message boards, locate the alphabet under the Surnames heading. Click the appropriate letter and then letter groupings to look through the lists of names. A yellow highlight shows you your current selections.

To browse localities or topics, scroll to the bottom of the Message Boards page. In the right-hand columns, you can see the number of sub-categories and boards associated with each topic. Click on a category to look through the available message boards.

Localities Categories		
Category	Sub-Categories	Boards
Australia	8	2
Canada	14	2
United Kingdom and Ireland	6	1
United States	2	1
Western Europe	14	0
>> More Localities Categories		
Topics Categories		
Category	Sub-Categories	Boards
Cemeteries & Tombstones	7	2
Genealogy Software	0	14
Immigration and Emigration	6	8
Military	13	8
Research Resources	5	16
>> More Topics Categories		

The browse view of message boards for localities and topics.

And don't worry about getting lost as you browse. You can always identify where you are in the Message Board hierarchy by looking under the Message Boards heading at the top of the page; you'll see the path you took to get to the page you are presently viewing. For example: *Boards >Localities > North America > United States >States>Ohio*. You can click on any of these linked topics to return to that category or subcategory.

Advanced Searching

The advanced search can be used to narrow down searches by subject line, the author of the message, and more. To do an advanced search, click the **Message Boards** tab, then click the "Advanced Search" link at the top of the page.

Advanced Search

Tip: Visit the Board FAQ for tips on how to make your searches more effective.

Name or Keyword	[ ]
Subject of Message	[ ]
Author of Message	[ ]
Last Name (surname)	[ ] ☐ Use Soundex
Message Classification	All ⌄
Posted Within	Anytime ⌄

Search

Advanced search options

Complete any of these fields as necessary:

In this field	Do this
Name or Keyword	Enter a keyword or phrase. Any message that contains this keyword or phrase will appear in the search results.
Subject of Message	Enter a keyword or phrase. Any message which has this keyword on phrase in its subject line will appear in the search results.
Author of Message	Enter the name of a message board poster.
Last Name (surname)	Enter a surname (last name or family name). Any message that contains this name in the Surnames field will appear in the search results. Make sure to try different spellings, including spacing variations (van Horn and vanhorn, or O'Brien and OBrien).
Use Soundex	Click the checkbox so that the search will find surnames with the same Soundex code.

In this field	Do this
Message Classification	Choose a message type from the drop-down list.
	A user is required to select one of these classifications each time he or she makes a post. Choose "All" to search through all available messages regardless of the message classification.
Posted Within	Choose an option from the drop-down list to restrict your search to messages that have been posted within a certain period of time. Choose "Anytime" to search through all available message boards.

Tips for Successful Searches

If your searches haven't turned up the results you were hoping for, try some of these search tips:

- Use wildcards—wildcards are special symbols (such as the asterisk "*" and the question mark "?") that are used in searching to represent unknown letters in a word. Use the asterisk to find words that begin with the same letters. Enter at least the first three letters of the word , followed by an asterisk. For example, a search for "Joh*" will return matches such as John, Johns, or Johnson. "Peter*" will give you results including Peter, Peters, Peterson, Petersen, and Peterman. Use the question mark for names that differ only by one letter. For example, a search for "Johns?n" will return both "Johnsen" and "Johnson."

- If you're using the Advanced Search option, try entering information in fewer fields or search only by a surname or keyword. This will broaden your search and return more matches.

  If the surname you are looking for is also a common word (such as Hill), use the Last Name (surname) field in the Advanced Search option. This enables you to search only message board posts in which this "word" is used as a surname and eliminates authors' names from coming up in your results.

Navigating Through the Boards

Now that you've found a message board you're interested in investigating, the next step is to look for messages that might be relevant to your family and your research interests. At the top of the message board, you will see the name of the board and also the number of total messages on the board and the number of threads (messages that have been replied to and have started a discussion). Here's an example of a surname message board:

Author—The name of the individual (not user name) who posted the message. You can click on this link to the poster's contact e-mail and view his or her public profile (if the user has chosen to make them available).

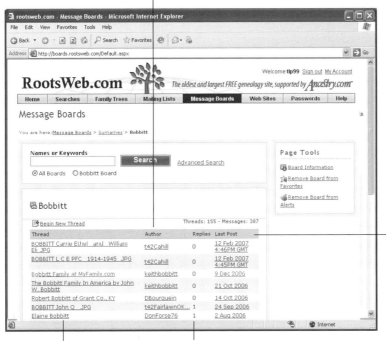

Last Post—The date when the message was posted; for threads with multiple postings, the date of the last message.

Thread—The subject line of a message posted to the board.

Replies—The number of replies that the message has received.

> Note: You can always return to the main message board page to navigate to other message boards by clicking the "Message Boards" link or tab at the top of the page. You can also use the two search boxes to access other message boards or simply narrow your search within the message board you're currently accessing.

If you find a subject line that gets your attention, you can click the link to go to that specific message. And remember, most message boards have multiple pages, so don't forget to use the "<<Previous" and "Next>>" links at the bottom of the board to navigate to other pages of messages.

You can look at messages in either thread view or flat view. Here's how the display options work:

Thread view is the default view. In this view, the entire original message (or post) is displayed at the top of the page. Replies to the message (its subject line, author, and date) are listed below according to the date they were posted, from earliest to most recent. To view the full text of any of the replies, click on the subject line and the full message appears.

To switch to the flat view, click the "Change to Flat View"

Thread view of a message board post

link below the original message. In the flat view, messages are displayed in the same order as the thread view (with the original post at the top and replies listed underneath), but the full text of each message is visible so that you can scan the full text of all the messages at one time.

Posting Your Own Messages: When, Where, and How

Found a new ancestor? Want to post a message about a family line you are researching or want to share a document that you've discovered? Naturally, your goal is to reach the greatest number of interested researchers as possible. Posting your own queries on the RootsWeb message boards is an excellent way to find others who are researching the same families and who may have the information you seek.

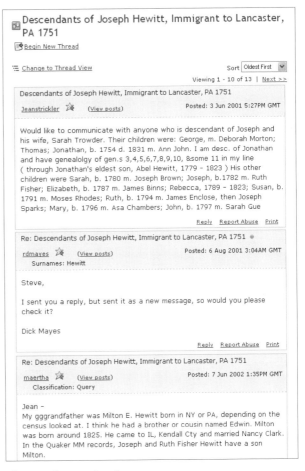

Flat view of message board post

Create an Effective Message

Today's online researchers are busy people, so you want to make sure that your message is posted to a relevant message board and is easy to understand. Does your message primarily concern a surname or single family? Then post it on the message board for that surname. If it pertains to several families or generations all living in the same geographic area, post on a specific locality message board. If your message is more closely tied to a research topic such as an ethnic group or occupation, you may elect to post on a message board for that topic.

Now that you've chosen the most appropriate board to post to, you're ready to write your message. To post a brand-new message, click the "Begin New Thread" link at the top of a message board. To respond to a specific message, click the "Reply" link located at the bottom of the message. If you reply to a post, it will be "threaded" with the message to which you are replying. Threading means that responses are grouped with the original message rather than standing alone as an original post. Posting a response (reply) to an original message also means that if the previous posters in the thread have elected to receive e-mail notification of responses, they will be notified of your new message.

The most important element of your message may be the subject line. The subject line catches people's attention and determines whether they will read the rest of your message. Make the subject line complete, concise, and try to cover the basics of who, when, and where. Do not use vague subjects such as "genealogy," "searching," or "looking for grandfather." You can assume that anyone posting or reading these message boards is searching for genealogy-related information.

Here is an example of how to create a good subject line. If you are posting a query about John Smith who was born in 1832 in Pittsburgh, a bad subject line would be: Looking for Smith family history. An informative subject line would be: John SMITH, born 1832, Pittsburgh, Pennsylvania." After you write a subject line, put yourself in the place of someone scanning through hundreds of posts on the message boards.

Does your subject line identify the content of your message? If it doesn't, consider rewriting it.

When you're posting a message, you can further help users locate your query by completing the Surnames field. Users can use the message board's Advanced Search to specifically search this field for surnames. Enter *only* the surnames that you have included in this message; do not include other surnames just because you are researching them. List surnames one at a time and separate them with a comma. For example, enter "Smith, Cousins, James, Kohlhammer, Van Allen." It doesn't matter whether you list the names in upper, lower, or mixed case but surnames that have common spelling variants such as Wood and Woods should be listed separately and not as Wood(s) or Wood/Woods.

Tips for Successful Posts

To make your posts as effective as possible, read through these tips:

- Don't post messages that are offensive, contain advertisements, or infringe on copyrights—these posts will be removed immediately.

- Message boards are read and used by researchers around the world, so watch those abbreviations. Don't assume everyone knows where or what "SF, CA" is. If in doubt, spell it out.

- Resist impulse posting. Take a few moments to think about your query before you post. Planning ahead helps avoid the embarrassment that a hastily prepared, poorly thought-out, query can sometimes cause (like mixing up your family names, giving the wrong dates, and misspelling words).

Add an Attachment

To use the message boards to their fullest potential, you might want to consider adding an attachment to your message. Certain types of attachments—GEDCOM files and graphic files, including pictures and scanned images—may be attached to any board message. The potential uses of such attachments are endless. Post a transcription of a will, deed, or family Bible record and add a scan of the image of the original record for others to view and download. Maybe you have unidentified family photos you would like to upload so that others might view, and possibly identify, the people in the pictures. And, in addition to posting a query, you can attach a GEDCOM of your family tree that may be downloaded by other researchers.

To add an attachment, click the "Attach a file" link at the bottom of the message and select the file you want to attach to the post. The files will be accessible when anyone views your message.

Correct a Message—After It's Been Posted

After you have posted a message, you may learn that the information in your message is incorrect or perhaps you are no longer interested in researching the line you mentioned. Whatever the reason, you have a couple options that will help you "correct" your original message. If you want to completely remove the post, you will need to enlist the help of the board's administrator; click the "Report Abuse" link in the message you want to delete. Explain why you want the post removed and include the fact that you are the author of the message. Another option is to "update" the post. You can do this by posting a follow-up response to your original message. While viewing the message, click the "Reply" link and list any additional information you have obtained or clarify any

mistakes. Anyone who finds your original message will also find your update.

Requesting a New Board

Don't see a message board for a surname or topic you're interested in? Although there are thousands and thousands of message boards, you may be interested in a subject that doesn't currently have a suitable message board. You may request a board for a new genealogical research topic, locality, or a surname of interest to you.

Click the **Message Boards** tab; then, click the "Request New Board" link at the bottom of the page. Enter a name for the message board and also any information about what you would like the board to contain, who it would be of interest to, etc. If you would like to be the board's administrator, you can indicate that on the submission form by click the "I would like to administer this board" checkbox. You will be notified by e-mail when your request has been approved or denied.

Adopting a Board

A message board administrator assists other users; promotes interest in the board; and is responsible for monitoring the board and deleting messages that break copyrights, are offensive, or violate the Board Rules. If you want to participate in the RootsWeb community, one way to start is to adopt a board and become an administrator. To find out more about the duties of a message board administrator, visit <http://ancboards. rootsweb.com/mbexec.xc?htx=admin.help&r=rw>.

To determine if a board needs an administrator, look for a "Volunteer to Admin" link in the Page Tools on the right-hand side of a message board page. Click this link and submit your request; you will be notified by e-mail when your request has been approved or denied.

Message board Page Tools

Your Message Board Preferences

If you are a registered user at RootsWeb, you can create a public profile and have your own personalized favorites and alert lists for message boards.

The public profile is a way to tell others about yourself and your research interests. If you choose to create a public profile, it will be linked to your public posts on RootsWeb such as WorldConnect trees, User-Submitted Databases, and Message Board posts.

If you are experiencing difficulties with this page or think you have uncovered a bug, contact the HelpDesk. If you have feedback on this feature, please email feedback@rootsweb.com.

About Me

Know the rules:
- 200 words max.
- **DO NOT** use abusive, adult-oriented, obscene or otherwise offensive language.
- **DO NOT** mention full names (unless deceased), email or street addresses, phone numbers or personal URLs.

RootsWeb is a family web site - please respect the Community Guidelines.

Upload a Photo [ ] Browse...

(.jpg, .gif, or .png files under 8 MB in size. Your photo will be resized to a maximum of 100 px wide or tall.)

Family History Experience

Researching Since [ ] (e.g. 1978)
Experience Level [Not Specified]
Research Frequency [Not Specified]

Basic Information

Country [Choose country...]
State/Province/County [ ]
City [ ]
Gender [Not Specified]
Age Group [Not Specified]
Education [Not Specified]
Employment Status [Not Specified]
Occupation [Not Specified]
Religion [Not Specified]
Languages [Add a Language] **Add**

Public Profile options

Create or Update Your Public Profile

A public profile lets you tell others about your interests so that people with similar interests can find you. The more information you add to your profile, the better your chances of connecting with someone. The profile you create will be linked to all your public posts in the message boards—and to your WorldConnect trees and any databases you submit.

You can create or update your profile by clicking the "My Public Profile" link available at the top, right-hand side of any message board page.

{ Note: To view another member's public profile, click their user name, located at the top of any message board post.

Bookmark Your Favorites

If you find a message board that you are interested in and want
to return to often, you can add it to a list of your favorites.
Simply click the "Add Board to Favorites" link in the Page Tools
on the right-hand side of the page. (You can also add specific
threads of messages to your favorites; click the "Add Thread to
Favorites" link in the Page Tools.) Then, to access a complete
list of quick links to your favorites, click the "My Favorites"
link at the top of any message board page.

{ Note: You can also make the author of a specific
message a favorite.

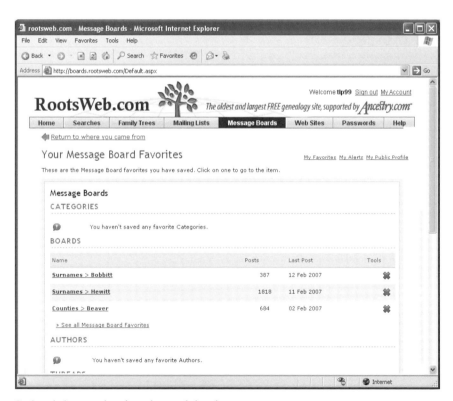

Bookmarked message boards, authors, and threads

Receive Alerts

If you want, you can be sent e-mail alerts about the message boards: when someone replies to a message you've posted (click the "Send me an alert" checkbox on the message) or when new messages are posted to your favorite board (click the "Add Board to Alerts" link in the Page Tools on the right-hand side of the page).

To see a complete list of the alerts you have signed up for, click the "My Alerts" link at the top of any message board page.

Your selected message board alerts

Family Bible Finds Its Way Home

By Anita Clayton,
RootsWeb User

One June, I received an e-mail from Jack Davis of Pennington, New Jersey, that made me hyperventilate with excitement. He said he had found a posting of mine at RootsWeb.

The message was one I had put on the NJMonmou-L (Monmouth County, New Jersey) mailing list and mentioned my third great-grandmother, Mary Ann CONK (born 1803), and her husband, Hezekiah AYRES (born 1797), who lived near Crosswicks, near the border of Burlington and Mercer counties in New Jersey.

He wrote, "Over the weekend I purchased a small family Bible from the 1860s in a box lot at an auction near Crosswicks. It is Mary Ann (CONK) AYRES's Bible, and lists her children (with birth dates) and also mentions that she is the daughter of John and Sarah CONK." He had done a Google search on AYRES and CONK and found my old message in archives for the list. All the details fit.

"If you're interested in having it, I'd be happy to mail it to you in the next week or two," he wrote. Well, of course I was interested. "I don't want anything for it," he continued, "I paid very little and it would be fun to reunite it with a family member, especially since I'm also interested in genealogy."

A couple of weeks later, I went to Trenton and met him on the front steps of the New Jersey State Archives, which is near his job. He handed me the small, worn, but well-preserved Bible that had been given to my third great-grandmother more than 150 years ago.

Making Connections with Mailing Lists

Whether you are a brand-new researcher or a more experienced one, mailing lists are one of the best vehicles for finding information about your ancestors and locating cousins or others who may be able to help you. Mailing lists are also great for in-depth group discussions and often appeal to those with a serious interest in a particular subject. RootsWeb currently hosts about 30,000 mailing lists (the number grows weekly) pertaining to different surnames, localities, and other useful genealogical-related topics such as occupations, fraternal organizations, religions, and even heraldry and royalty.

So how do mailing lists work? A member of the list sends an e-mail to the mailing list's e-mail address, and the list retransmits (or sends) the message to everyone who is subscribed to that particular list. The list keeps you in contact constantly with dozens, even hundreds, of other family history enthusiasts who share your specific interests.

You can simply monitor a list for names, dates, and facts that will help jump-start your research, or you can post your own questions periodically to increase your chances of finding information you need to be successful with your research.

The RootsWeb mailing lists are divided into four main categories: surnames, United States localities, international localities, and special interests. Surnames are broken down alphabetically; U.S. localities are separated by general interests and states, counties, and even districts; international localities are broken down by country, with some larger countries being further split by smaller areas; and the special interest mailing lists contain hundreds of topics, including prisons, occupations, ethnicities, and organizations.

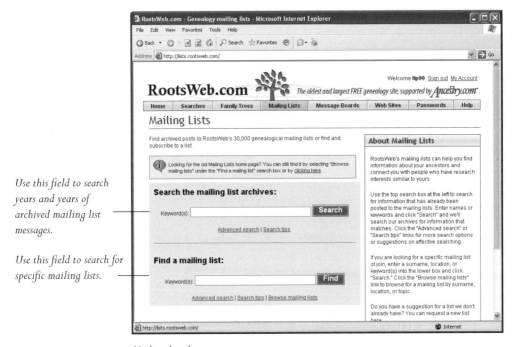

Use this field to search years and years of archived mailing list messages.

Use this field to search for specific mailing lists.

Mailing lists homepage

Exploring the Mailing Lists

Before you join a mailing list, you can browse the entire
collection to see which topics and lists interest you most. Click
the **Mailing Lists** tab at the top of any RootsWeb page or go
to <http://lists.rootsweb.com>. At the bottom of the page, click
the "Browse mailing lists" link or go to <http://lists.rootsweb.
com/index/index.html>. Now you can navigate through the
boards by clicking on category and sub-category folders. The
top of the page of most mailing lists, you should see the name
of the mailing list and the topic that it covers. For example, the
ethnic-welsh mailing list, "PA-WELSH-EARLY-L," is a mailing
list for anyone with a genealogical interest in the Welsh who
settled in southeastern Pennsylvania prior to 1750.

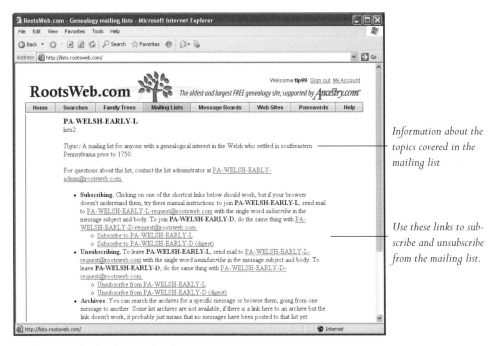

Information about the topics covered in the mailing list

Use these links to sub-scribe and unsubscribe from the mailing list.

The homepage for the ethnic mailing list, PA-WELSH-EARLY-L

Search for a Specific List

In addition to looking through the index of mailing lists, you can search for specific mailing lists using keywords, locations, surnames, and even categories. To search for a specific list, click the **Mailing Lists** tab. In the "Find a mailing list" section, enter a keyword. The search engine will return mailing lists that use this keyword in their name. You can also click the "Advanced search link" to narrow your search: search for a list based on its name or description; search for lists that focus on specific states and countries; or search for surnames in a specific mailing list. If you are having trouble finding the list you're looking for, try searching using the Description field only.

Keyword		Advanced
List Name:		
Description:		
Country:		
State:		
County:		
Surname:		
Category:		
Search Search tips		

Mailing lists Advanced Search

Tips for Successful Searches

You can use basic Boolean search terms and wildcards to help locate the exact mailing lists posts you're looking for:

- Search for an entire phrase by putting quotes around the group of words, like "john jones."

- Use "AND" to require the search to find all words or phrases—"john AND jones" will return only results with both words.

- Use "NOT" to exclude words or phrases—for example, "john NOT jones" will return all results that contain the word john but not jones.

- Use wildcards—wildcards are special symbols (such as the asterisk "*" and the question mark "?") that are used in searching to represent unknown letters in a word. Use the asterisk to find words that begin with the same letters. Enter at least the first three letters of the name, followed by an asterisk. For example, a search for "Jon*" will return matches such as Jon, Jones, or Jonson. Use the question mark for names that differ only by one letter. For example, a search for "J?nes" will return both "Jones" and "Janes."

Mining the Archives

The RootsWeb mailing lists archives contain the content of years of discussions that have been carried on among researchers of the subject matter of these various mailing lists. Buried in these archives could be some treasures that might benefit you in your quest to learn more about your ancestors. Someone at another time—perhaps years ago—might have posted just the information you seek today.

To begin a search of the archives, click the **Mailing Lists** tab. In the "Search the mailing list archives" section, enter a keyword or name. The search engine will search *all* of the mailing lists at one time—instead of one at a time—and will look for this keyword in the subject line or body of posts. You can also click the "Advanced search" link to narrow your search: search for a post on a certain day, month, or year; search for a keyword in a specific mailing list; or search for a specific person's post using their e-mail address. If you want to search the archives of a specific mailing list, access the mailing list and click either the "Search the archives" link or the "Browse the archives" link.

{ **Note: The search tips explained earlier in the chapter also work when searching the mailing list archives.**

Keyword	Advanced

Body:	
Subject:	
From:	
	(email address of poster)
List:	
	(limit search to one mailing list)
Date:	
	(e.g. 10 Jun 2005, Jun 2005, or 2005)

Search Search tips

Advanced Search for the mailing lists archives

Joining a Mailing List

You can subscribe to (join) a mailing list at any time—and subscribe to as many as you'd like. First, use the searching techniques discussed earlier in the chapter to find a mailing list of interest; then, click on its link. The page that appears will tell you the name of the mailing list and what topics the list covers. Below this information are links that subscribe you to the list. You can choose from two types of e-mail distribution—regular mail mode and a digest (D) mode. The mail mode sends single e-mail messages to each subscriber as they are posted. The digest mode sends each subscriber the messages, but they are saved up and then sent out as a group. On large and busy mailing lists, you might want to use the digest mode. On the other hand, some ISPs (Internet Service Providers) have a problem with large digests, so the mail mode might work better. Sometimes you have to experiment to find the right mailing lists and the right mode. You can even try both modes to see which works for you.

To subscribe to the mailing list, click either the mail or digest (D) "Subscribe to" link. An e-mail message appears. Make sure the word "Subscribe" is in the subject line and the body of the message; then send the e-mail. It's that simple. You should receive a welcome e-mail to let you know that you have successfully subscribed to the list.

One nice option of mailing lists is that you can unsubscribe and subscribe as often as necessary. For example, when you take vacation you might want to unsubscribe from the list so your messages don't pile up and then re-subscribe when you return—make sure to search the mailing list's archives to be sure you didn't miss something important while you were away. To unsubscribe from the mailing list, access the right mailing list and click one of the "Unsubscribe from" links. An e-mail message appears. Make sure the word "Unsubscribe" is in the subject line of the message; then send the e-mail.

Posting a Message

Besides acquiring information from others interested in the same topics, mailing lists are a great place to post your own information, questions, and comments. Don't be a genealogy bystander, get involved. Sending a post is as easy as sending an e-mail. First, make sure you have subscribed to the list. Open an e-mail and in the address field, enter the list's name in this format: listname@rootsweb.com. For example, if the mailing list's name is "Bobbitt," then you would enter: bobbitt@rootsweb.com. Make sure the body of the e-mail is just plain text, not HTML so it will be readable. Also, because this e-mail message will go to everyone on the mailing list, potentially thousands of people, don't include any information in the e-mail that you don't want everyone else to see.

Starting a Mailing List

Don't see the mailing list you want? You can start one, but first double-check to see if the name, location, or subject is already covered by another list. To request a new mailing list, go to the homepage and find the "Mailing Lists" section, then click the "Requests for Mailing Lists" link or go to <http://resources.rootsweb.com/cgi-bin/listrequest.pl>. Enter your contact information and details about the new list, and submit the form.

> Note: If you request a new mailing list, you will automatically become its administrator. If you do not want to be a list's administrator, do not request a list.

You can also "adopt" a list you're interested in if it doesn't already have an administrator. You do not need any special equipment other than Internet access to become a list administrator—even public access to the Internet at a local library works. Your responsibilities will include removing bad e-mail addresses, assisting list users with their questions, and resolving any problems. To find out more about a mailing list administrator's responsibilities, visit <http://helpdesk.rootsweb.com/listadmins>.

The ROOTS-L Mailing List

Among the numerous mailing lists available on RootsWeb is ROOTS-L. This mailing list started back in 1987 and is *the* original genealogy mailing list on the Internet. (And actually, it is more or less the formal start of RootsWeb.) For those who are interested in any or all aspects of genealogy, this mailing list is a resource you won't want to pass up. To subscribe to the ROOTS-L mailing list, access the homepage, find the "Mailing List" section, and click the "ROOTS-L Mailing List" link or go to <http://www.rootsweb.com/roots-l>. A word of caution: thousands and thousands of people subscribe and respond to this mailing list so be prepared for lots of e-mail! You can also search more than ten years of archived ROOTS-L messages from users all over the world at <http://listsearches.rootsweb.com/cgi-bin/listsearch.pl?list=ROOTS>.

Cooking Up a Family Reunion

By Pamela Burnette,
RootsWeb User

If you've done genealogy for some time I'm sure you've had a serendipitous find in a library or cemetery as you look for some clue—any clue—to your family tree. I recently had a serendipitous find of my own, and all because of a fund-raising cookbook project for the Claiborne County, Tennessee Cemetery Association. The cookbook, "Don't Stand in the Sun with Butter on Your Head," has sold better than I ever dreamed thanks to the support of the folks on the Claiborne County mailing list and the people that read about it in the local Tennessee newspaper.

We had two orders for the book from Monroe, Michigan, both of which were from people on the mailing list. When I received an order for a third book from Monroe, Michigan, I was quite surprised. The Tennessee newspaper article had reached the eyes of my stepmother via her mother who receives the paper and passes it on to share with her. When my stepmother ordered the cookbook there was no way for her to know that she was ordering it from me because the check and the order goes directly to the cemetery association.

However, I live in California and mail the cookbooks out from here. I knew as soon as she saw the return address she'd know who it was from. To save ya'll from my whole family history I'll just say that my brother and I have been estranged from my father's family all of our lives. I met him once and he wasn't interested, but I struck up a warm friendship with my stepmother. However, we lost track of one another and there's been no contact for probably twenty-five years.

I wrote her a short note, enclosed it with the cookbook, and sent it off. We've discovered we have two half-sisters that are as eager as are we to meet one another. My brother and I are old enough to be their parents but what the heck! Over a long three-day weekend, I'll go back to my brother's in Indiana and they'll come down to meet us. And all because of a cookbook that some of the folks on a RootsWeb mailing list contributed to so we could raise funds for a county cemetery association. Just goes to show you, what goes around comes around tenfold.

Volunteering: Ways to Make a Difference

One of the reasons RootsWeb has thrived year after year is because of caring people who are willing to help each other. RootsWeb hosts many of the largest volunteer genealogy projects on the Web. Individuals locate, transcribe, and publish genealogical data and help new users, all for free. Not only do these projects provide an enormous amount of information, they bring together a worldwide community of researchers with myriad backgrounds and various levels of expertise. It is this contact and exchange with fellow researchers that makes RootsWeb a great community.

Find something that interests you, contact the group, and get involved! You may be able to help someone with research in a particular state or county. And in return, someone else may be able to answer your questions about Swedish American research.

Volunteer Projects

RootsWeb is home to a number of large volunteer projects. (You can visit any of the projects by clicking on their links on the RootsWeb homepage.) Among the buried treasures one finds at RootsWeb are those created by various groups such as:

* The USGenWeb Project

* The WorldGenWeb Project

* FreeBMD (England and Wales)

* FreeReg (UK)

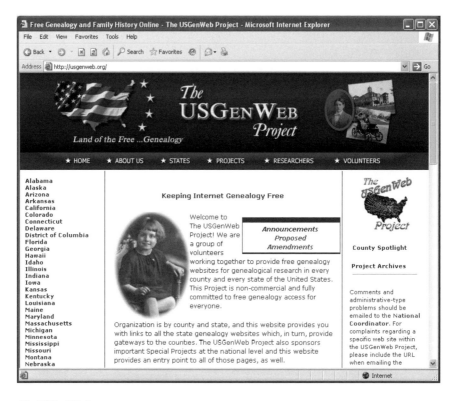

The USGenWeb homepage

The USGenWeb Project

The USGenWeb Project is a volunteer organization that is dedicated to keeping genealogy free using the Internet. They provide genealogical websites for every state and county in the United States. With fifty states and 3,100 counties, plus many independent cities and towns featuring websites, this huge project continues to grow and grow. Many of the websites offer marriage records, tombstone transcriptions, obituaries, and noteworthy family data—available nowhere else online. Many county sites also include interesting historical

The state website for Oregon on USGenWeb

information about the town including local histories and photographs. Have you ever wondered what Main Street of your ancestor's hometown in Kansas looked like in 1880? One of these sites just might show you.

To find out more about USGenWeb, go to the RootsWeb homepage and find the "Hosted Volunteer Projects" section, then click the "USGenWeb Project" link or go to <http://www.usgenweb.org>. On The USGenWeb Project page, you can access each state's homepage by clicking the links on the left-hand side of the page; from there you can navigate to any county in the state.

The USGenWeb Project also sponsors several focused projects of its own perhaps the most important being The USGenWeb Archives Project. The Archive's purpose it to collect and disseminate actual transcriptions of public records. Files are added daily and include everything from census records, pensions, and court cases, to church records and maps. Don't overlook this resource; you might find the record you've been looking for.

> Note: The information found for each state and county varies a great deal since each page is the creation of individual volunteers. You will find some sites that include the names of an entire county from the 1880 census and others that contain one family's cemetery records that an interested family member has submitted.

Volunteers for The USGenWeb Project can help in a variety of ways: coordinating county or state websites, transcribing records, doing "look-ups" for website users, and more. To offer your services, go to <http://www.usgenweb.org/volunteers/index.shtml>.

The WorldGenWeb Project

The WorldGenWeb Project is similar to USGenWeb, but its scope is broader. This volunteer-based project is dedicated to providing genealogical and historical records, and resources from countries around the world. For those who can't travel to their ancestral homelands, these records can be an invaluable resource. And for anyone nervous about venturing outside the United States, you'll be glad to know that any sites give you the option of viewing the site in English and the country's native language; don't let language barriers stop you from exploring a new avenue of research.

The WorldGenWeb homepage

Like The USGenWeb Project, The WorldGenWeb also has an Archives Project. However, the Archives currently contain very few records for very few countries. To find out more about The WorldGenWeb Project, go to the RootsWeb homepage and find the "Hosted Volunteer Projects" section, then click the "WorldGenWeb Project" link or go to <http://worldgenweb.org>.

FreeBMD (England and Wales)

FreeBMD stands for Free Births, Marriages, and Deaths. This project's objective is to transcribe the Civil Registration index of births, marriages, and deaths for England and Wales and provide free Web access to the information. (The Civil Registration system for recording births, marriages, and deaths in England and Wales has been in place since 1837 and is one of the most significant single resources for genealogical research back through Victorian times.) FreeBMD currently features more than 126 million records for 1837–1983. And best of all, you can view images of the original documents.

Image of a birth record in FreeBMD

To search the records, go to the homepage and find the "Hosted Volunteer Projects" section, then click the "FreeBMD" link or go to <http://freebmd.rootsweb.com>. If you want to volunteer to transcribe records, go to <http://freebmd.rootsweb. com/Signup.html>.

FreeREG

FreeREG stands for Free Registers. The overall aim of Free Registers is to provide baptism, marriage, and burial records that have been extracted from the parish registers and non-conformist church records in the United Kingdom. (Recording baptisms, marriages, and burials in parish registers began in 1538.) Because FreeREG is a relatively new project, only a bit more than a million records are included. To search the records, go to the homepage and find the "Hosted Volunteer Projects" section, then click the "FreeReg" link or go to <http:// freereg.rootsweb.com>.

Contributions, whether small or large, help the database grow and become an essential and valuable tool to all those who are researching their ancestry in the United Kingdom. Volunteers are needed to transcribe the registers, county coordinators can help obtain the data, and programmers keep the information flowing smoothly. If you want to help out, go to <http://freereg.rootsweb.com/volunteers/index.htm>.

Other Hosted Volunteer Projects

Here are some other valuable volunteer projects that are hosted by RootsWeb and its community of volunteers. They can be found on the homepage in the "Hosted Volunteer Projects" section.

- **Books We Own.** This project contains a virtual library of books that volunteers either own or have access to and are willing to look up information for you.

- **The Obituary Daily Times.** This index of published obituaries is published daily from newspapers in the U.S., England, and Canada.

User-Contributed Databases

The user-contributed databases are collections of records compiled by volunteers from a variety of sources. More than 11 million names appear in these files from all over the world and the collection continues to grow. Each user-contributed data collection offers unique and valuable material that is available nowhere else. For example, on Saibai Island, a remote area in the Torres Strait located between New Guinea and Cape York Peninsula of northeast Australia, a woman has compiled more than 171,000 records of genealogical interest that she painstakingly culled from the *Creswick and Clunes Advertiser,* the agricultural journal of Talbot County, Victoria, Australia, dating from May 1849 to December 1865. Keep in mind, however, that few of these databases are as comprehensive in records and names as this example.

Thousands of other generous researchers across the world have gathered similar difficult-to-obtain genealogical information and made it publicly available in these user-contributed databases for the use of family historians everywhere. Categories range from book indexes and church records, to mortality schedules and Native American records. You'll also find many databases organized by locality or ethnic group.

Search the Databases

The good news about these user-contributed databases is that your ancestors' names may be listed among them. The bad news is that you cannot find them by conducting one general search. Instead, you have to search each database one by one.

So the first step to finding your family is to find a database that might be relevant to your family history. Databases are grouped together in categories to make this easier for you.

To explore the different types of databases available, click the **Searches** tab and look for the "User Contributed Records—Databases" section. You will see links for different types of records, both for the United States and on an international level. When you click on a link, you will see search fields for that specific group of databases.

Database = Marriage Records

Marriage Record for James H. BOBBITT

Spouse: <u>Mildred M. Trinkle</u>
Date: 28 Jun 1922
B/G: Groom
Born: 28 February 1901
Source: Book:21 Page:12
County and State: Orange Co. IN
Notes:
Groom ethnicity = White.
Bride ethnicity = White.

Discrepancies were discovered when comparing the bride index with the groom index. Notes have been added to individual records, when applicable, to identify discrepancies or provide information found in other resources (i.e., census records).

User-Added Notes (<u>click here</u> to add a note):
   none

A search result from the Marriage Records user-contributed databases

How You Can Help

You know the "why" behind contributing a database. But do you know the "what" and "how?" Only a small fraction of genealogy-related information is on the Web. Most of it is in the form of books, documents (many handwritten), photographs, microfilm, and microfiche held by tens of thousands of libraries; genealogy societies; churches; local, state, and national government archives; and other organizations.

Databases can be created from all sorts of lists. For example, did your dad serve in the Korean War or WWII, or was your grandfather in WWI? Did any of them keep papers stored away at home—a roster of those friends with whom they had been stationed? Perhaps they attended reunions with their Army buddies and brought home a list of those in attendance? Such information would be of great value to others searching RootsWeb for their family members. You can use the RootsWeb user-contributed databases as a place to make the information publicly-available; you just might have the key to unlock someone else's pedigree.

You do not need fancy or difficult-to-understand software to prepare your information for submission. Create a simple text file by typing the data directly into whatever word-processing program you normally use—Word, Word Perfect, Works, or even the Windows WordPad program. You can find guidelines and examples at <http://userdb.rootsweb.com/guidelines.html> and even a tutorial at <http://userdb.rootsweb.com/submit/tutorial.html>.

Other Ways to Share Your Research with the Community

The hundreds of gigabytes of data on RootsWeb are a byproduct of millions of online genealogists sharing their research. Here are some ways you can contribute, too:

- Upload your family tree to RootsWeb WorldConnect. Even though your tree may be small at first, by adding it to WorldConnect, others can find you and share connections. The more you share, the more likely someone else will be able to find that illusive connection and share their data with you.

- Post your family surnames on the RootsWeb Surname List (RSL). The RSL is a registry of more than 1 million surname entries that have been submitted by more than 238,000 online genealogists. Associated with each surname are dates, locations, and information about how to contact the person who submitted the surname. The RSL is one of the primary tools on RootsWeb that online genealogists use to contact each other and share information.

- Join a mailing list or post a message to a message board. Not only can you post a question there, but perhaps you will be able to answer someone else's questions. It is also a way to share data so that others can find it. Everyone was a "newbie" once. So even if you can't help anyone else now, six months from now, you may be able to return the favor and help someone else get started.

- Add Post-em notes—electronic sticky notes—to the Social Security Death Index (SSDI), WorldConnect, or other databases at RootsWeb. You can help the poster correct errors, add links to relevant websites, or simply let them know that you have additional information they could be looking for.

- Request a freepage and build your own genealogy website. You may provide the information that others just like you are looking for. If you already have a website, you can also link this site to a relevant surname or location.

Christmas Arrived Early

By Marian Presswood,
RootsWeb User

I am the lone caregiver for my ninety-two-year-old mom who is in the late stages of Alzheimer's disease. She was never really interested in family history, but now she is unable to speak and the terrible disease has robbed her of any precious family memories that she might have been willing to share.

She told me once, years ago, that although she had no pictures of her grandfather John C. PORTER, she saw him a few times as a small child on summer vacation visits and that he was a courtly gentleman with white hair, beard, and mustache and always wore a suit with a white shirt and tie.

As the official county historian and president of the local historical and genealogical society, I had submitted quite a bit of information to online county websites, but had little time to surf the genealogy sites. However, one July I made a quick check of the latest queries posted on the local RootsWeb county site and one jumped out at me that named all my mother's family surnames in bold headlines.

Needless to say, it only took me a few seconds to fire off a response to the submitter asking if we were related. It was almost as if she were right there waiting for me and when I told her who my great-grandfather was and that I had never seen a picture of him, she began scanning and sending images—not only of him, but of my great-grandmother, Lucy BROWN, my great-great-grandmother, Amanda BANKS Porter, my third great-grandmother, Martha WHISENANT Porter, and also letters written by my mother's sister almost forty years ago.

Wow! Talk about Christmas presents! It may have been July, but I don't think I've ever been as excited over any Christmas present as I was upon seeing those images appear on my computer screen that night.

A RootsWeb Essential

One of the many features available on RootsWeb is access to genealogy-related websites that have been created by organizations and individuals across the United States and the world. Some are created by RootsWeb users and hosted by the site and others are genealogy-related sites that have been created by individuals and families, associations, and counties and countries, and they are merely linked to RootsWeb. All of these websites hold a wealth of information and may be just the thing to build your family tree.

RootsWeb Freepages

In 1999, RootsWeb began offering free Web space—called freepages—to genealogists. Today, more than 11,000 individuals have taken advantage of this feature and store their family history or genealogy-related websites on RootsWeb. And you can too. Any user who requests an account and wants to create a website that fits within the parameters of RootsWeb is eligible for free, unlimited Web space. For those who can't afford to pay for their own Web space, the freepages are a valuable resource.

> Note: Websites cannot be used for personal photo albums, games, video or music files of any type, file storage, software, or commercial material. And absolutely no pornographic or adult-oriented material is permitted.

Request a Freepage

If you want to build a website on RootsWeb for your own family history or for your local genealogical society, you can request free space by clicking the **Web Sites** tab; then on the left-hand side of the page, click the "Request Free Web Space" link or go to <http://accounts.rootsweb.com>. There are three different types of space for your website that you can request: for personal use, for projects such as The USGenWeb Project, and for libraries and societies. Click the link for the type of page you want to create; accept the usage policy agreement, and you're ready to go.

> Note: RootsWeb used to provide special homepages for individuals that donated money to the website. This program is no longer available.

Set Up Your Site

You may have already created a Web page; if so, your setup is as easy as uploading your pages. However, you may need to create your website from scratch. Creating a basic Web page is not as difficult as you might imagine—many people have done it, thanks to easy-to-use HTML editing software. RootsWeb even offers a free online editor you can use if you don't already own the necessary software or you don't want to invest in a program. To access the online editor, click the **Help** tab. In the "Websites at RootsWeb & Web Authoring Tools" section at the bottom of the page, click the "Webmaster: Freepages Questions" link; then, click the "RootsWeb Online Editor" link. And if you need some guidance using the editor, go to <http://helpdesk.rootsweb.com/editor>.

In addition to the online editor, the HelpDesk at RootsWeb (accessible on the Help tab) gives you access to an abundance of information that can help you get your website up in no time. Go to <http://helpdesk.rootsweb.com/FAQ/fpindex.html> where you'll find basic instructions and tips; you can learn more about HTML, and get help with graphics and FTP programs—some users, in the true spirit of RootsWeb, have created their own freepage websites specifically to help new users create their own Web pages.

Search the Freepages

Although the information on freepages is included in the search results of the site-wide search engine, Search Thingy, you might also want to take a minute to browse the freepages and get familiar with what sites are out there. (For more information on Search Thingy, see page 12.) To view all the freepages alphabetically, go to the homepage and in the "Websites" section, click the "Websites on RootsWeb's Freepages" link or go to <http://freepages.rootsweb.com/directory/genealogy.html>.

If you want, you can also view the freepages grouped together by category (for example, military or alumni); click the **Web Sites** tab and in the "Surname Websites" section, click the "freepages indexes" link or go to <http://freepages.rootsweb. com/directory>.

One caveat to keep in mind: freepages are each named by the person who created them. That means when you're browsing through the lists, you might need to stretch your imagination to consider how others might label their own websites. Also be sure to look under generic terms such as ancestors, descendants, family, family history, family trees, genealogy, and homepages. Hundreds of sites are found under these categories that you might miss if you're strictly looking for specific surnames and alphabetical topics.

As you search or browse through the freepages, you'll notice that the websites reflect a broad range of interests and topics. Here are some examples of what you might find:

A freepage that focuses on Italian genealogy

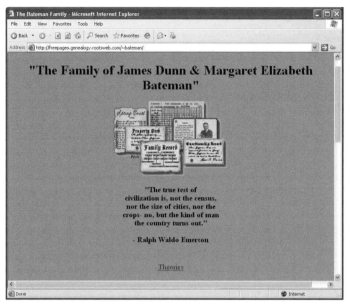

A freepage for a specific family line

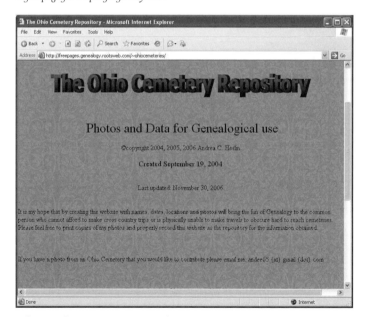

A freepage for cemetery records in Ohio

Registered Websites

Many organizations, genealogical societies, and individuals have created websites that contain family trees, databases, histories, and an almost endless amount of important family history information. Although some of these websites are *not* hosted by RootsWeb, they can still be linked to RootsWeb so that they are included in search results and users all over the world can have access to their information. (When you create a freepage it is automatically "registered." You don't need to register it again.)

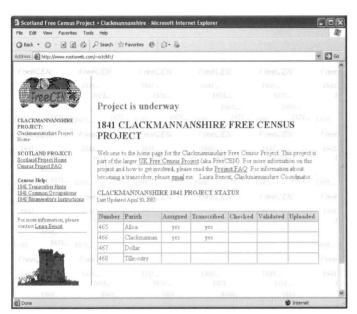

A registered website that contains Scottish census information

Register Your Website

If you want to link a website to RootsWeb, click the **Web Sites** tab, then on the top, left-hand side of the page, click the "Register Your Website" link. You can use this page to register websites that are housed at RootsWeb or other sites not located on RootsWeb. To register a website that is not affiliated with RootsWeb, click the "RootsLink" link at the bottom of the page or go to <http://resources.rootsweb.com/~rootslink/addlink.html>. You can choose which category you want your site registered under, including everything from fraternal organizations and books to sites that contain actual records.

Browse Registered Websites

Perhaps the easiest way to learn about sites that are linked to RootsWeb is to browse the various collections. To do so, click the **Web Sites** tab. You will see the different groups of websites including regional resources, surnames, major projects, and miscellaneous. Click each link to navigate through the groups.

The Social Security Death Index (SSDI) Goes International

By Elaine Holm,
RootsWeb User

I had no knowledge of any of my ancestors immigrating to the United States, but, late one night, I entered one of my surnames into the Social Security Death Index (SSDI) on RootsWeb. Imagine my shock and surprise at finding that one of my relatives had died in the United States.

That wasn't to be the end of my surprises with regard to this individual though. Two days later I received an e-mail in answer to a message I'd posted. It was from this particular individual's granddaughter. We have since been exchanging details and getting to know each other.

So my advice is to check everywhere. Someone might even have been visiting their homeland or have emigrated at census time. They might have died or married far from home.

Thank you for helping me find a cousin I didn't know about.

Cool Tools and Research Aids

RootsWeb has some cool tools to aid your research—
newsletters full of helpful hints and tips, charts to keep
your discoveries organized, an online library, a multitude of
resources to assist you in exploring your surname, and much
more. Make sure to take a few minutes and check out all of
RootsWeb and find your own favorite cool tools.

The *RootsWeb Review*

The *RootsWeb Review*, a free e-mail genealogy newsletter
sponsored by RootsWeb, rolled off the virtual press on 17
June 1998, and it has been published every week since then.
Each issue includes information about additions or changes
to RootsWeb (e.g., new databases and mailing lists), plus
instructions on using RootsWeb, readers' tips and stories,
and other articles of interest to family historians around the
world. To subscribe to the newsletter, go to the Newsletter
Management Center <http://newsletters.rootsweb.com> and enter

your e-mail address. You can also visit the management center to change the e-mail address to which the newsletter is sent or to unsubscribe from the newsletter.

If you haven't been a long-term subscriber to the newsletter, you can find every edition of the *RootsWeb Review* in the archives, a treasure trove of genealogical information. You can search for specific topics or browse through the archives by year, month, and date.

Charts and Forms

Almost nothing in family history research is as frustrating as following a great lead only to discover that you're really just finding the same information, the same website, or the same record—twice. RootsWeb has downloadable charts and forms that you can use to organize your research. Research calendars and extracts, source summaries, and correspondence records: all can help you keep track of your research paths. In addition, you'll find the most commonly used forms like ancestral (pedigree) charts, family group sheets, and census forms for the United States (1790–1930), the

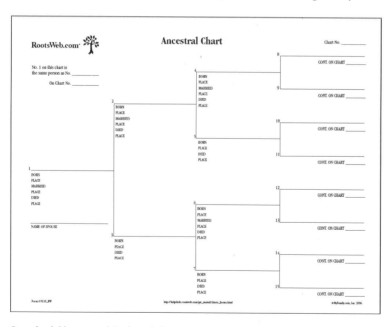

Downloadable ancestral (pedigree) chart

United Kingdom (1841–91), and Canada (1901 and 1911). You can link to these forms and others on the homepage; find the "Other Tools and Resources" section, then click the "Blank Charts and Forms" link or go to <http://helpdesk.rootsweb.com/ get_started/charts_forms.html>.

The Social Security Death Index (SSDI)

In the summer of 1935, President Roosevelt signed the Social Security Act into law; it was created to provide Social Security benefits to all eligible citizens. To assist in keeping track of individuals, the government assigns a numerical identification to each person involved in the program. Though it was originally intended for use within the Social Security Administration (SSA) only, its value as a unique identifier has promoted its application in other areas of society, such as drivers' license ID numbers, state and federal tax programs, motor vehicle registration, military ID (starting with the Vietnam era), etc. Since 1935, more than 370 million Social Security cards have been issued to the citizens and residents of the United States.

As a by-product of this vast recordkeeping system, the SSA developed a file of those individuals who received Social Security numbers and were reported as deceased. This file is the Social Security Death Master File. The Social Security Death Index (SSDI) on RootsWeb is generated from this Death Master File. You will find birth dates, death deaths, social security numbers, and the place of last residence. The database currently contains almost 80 million records.

Because the SSDI works best for finding information about individuals who died in the mid-1960s or later, this database often serves as a stepping stone to further research or as a verification of other sources. Also, the index can be of immense value for those who are for some reason unfamiliar with their parents or grandparents.

To search the SSDI, go to the homepage and find the "Search Engines and Databases" section, then click the "Social Security Death Index" link or go to <http://ssdi.rootsweb.com>.

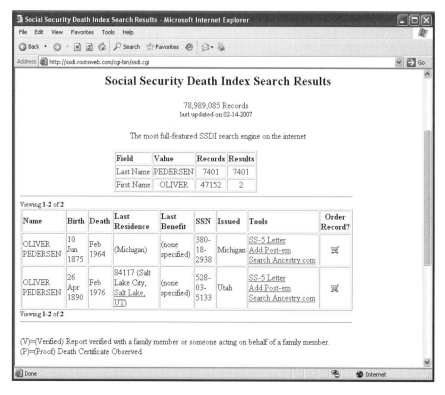

Search results for the SSDI

Limitations of the Database

If you don't see the family member you're looking for, there may be several logical reasons why you haven't found him or her in the database:

- Though the Social Security Act was created in 1935, a computer system for reporting death benefit claims did not exist until 1962; therefore, most of the names listed in the Social Security Death Index date from the 1960s. Although it is true that statistically the index contains a few individuals whose birth dates are listed as early as 1800, people who were born before 1860 comprise less than 0.00006% of the total entries in the index. Most of these entries are for persons who supposedly lived well past age 100, and are most likely the result of data-entry errors.

- Not all Americans were covered under the Social Security Act in its earlier days. Railroad workers, teachers, and other municipal employees often were covered by other retirement systems; therefore, the Social Security Administration did not record their information, and they might not be included in the SSDI.

- The entries in the index are overwhelmingly American; however, a few Canadians, Mexicans, and others are included in the database. If one is in the United States legally, one can obtain a Social Security card.

- If an individual's name and dates match your ancestor but the "last residence" doesn't, remember that the last residence may not be the actual place of death, especially if an individual died in an out-of-town hospital, on vacation, etc. The last residence is more properly the last "address of record." Also consider the possibility that a person might have had more than one official residence as many "snowbirds" do.

U.S. Town/County Database

Because many government records in the United States are stored on the county level, you'll want to find the state, county, and town for important events in your ancestors' lives. For example, if your grandmother told you that she and grandpa were married in Bowlegs, Oklahoma, the easy way to learn the name of the county is to use the U.S. Town / County Database <http://resources.rootsweb.com/cgi-bin/townco.cgi>. Type in "Bowlegs" and include the abbreviation of the state, "OK."

Results for City: nyssa

City	State	County
Nyssa	OR	Malheur
Nyssa	MO	Butler
NyssaHeights	OR	Malheur

Town Name (required)

nyssa

State Abbreviation (optional)

Submit Query

U.S. Town / County Database search results

Up pops the answer: Seminole County. Now you know where to go to find your grandparents' marriage record.

As another example, if you have an obituary that indicates your ancestor died in Paradise Valley, type in the town's name, "Paradise Valley," and you'll discover that there are four towns in four different states with this name. You now know which states to focus your search on.

Soundex Converter

Soundex is a special coding system that is used for searching the indexes of many U.S. censuses and ship passenger lists. The purpose of Soundex is to identify names that have similar pronunciations but different spellings; it helps not only with spelling variations but with transcription errors. Each surname is assigned a code that consists of a letter (the first letter of the name) followed by three numbers representing the consonants. As search engines have become more sophisticated, the need for Soundex search capabilities has lessened. However, Soundex searches are still available for several RootsWeb databases. In addition, you can utilize the RootsWeb Soundex Converter <http://resources.rootsweb.com/cgi-bin/soundexconverter> to aid your research by identifying spelling variations for a given surname. For example, if you are searching for an ancestor with the last name of "Pedersen," type the surname in the Soundex Converter and you'll discover that Paterson, Peterson, and Peterssen are all variations of the Pedersen surname. In databases that don't allow Soundex searching, you can try out these name variations yourself.

RootsWeb's Soundex Converter

Click Here to insert this searchbox into your webpage.

The Soundex system is a method of indexing names in the 1880, 1900, 1910, and 1920 US Census. Soundex can also aid genealogists by identifying spelling variations for a given surname.

This form will return the soundex code for the entered surname, plus other surnames/spellings sharing the same soundex code.

Surname: pedersen   [Get Soundex Code]

Soundex Code for pedersen = P362

Other surnames sharing this Soundex Code:
PATERSON | PATRICK | PATRIS | PATTERSON | PEDERSEN | PEDERSON | PETERS | PETERSDOTTER | PETERSEN | PETERSON | PETERSSEN | PETERSSON | PETROSKY | PIETERS | PIOTROSKI | PODRAZA | POYTHRESS |

Back to http://resources.rootsweb.com/cgi-bin/soundexconverter

Soundex Converter search results

The RootsWeb Surname List (RSL)

The RootsWeb Surname List is a registry of more than one million surnames that have been submitted by tens of thousands of researchers who are actively working on their family lines. A unique feature of RSL is that each surname is associated with dates and locations. You can search for surnames, and if they also include the same area and similar time frame you're interested in, you can contact the person who submitted the surname. Remember, just because someone is researching the same surname you are, that doesn't necessarily mean they are related to you or are looking for the same ancestral lines. If you're researching the surname "Woodbury" and your family of this name lived in Alabama in the 1800s, a person with information on the English Woodbury family who lived in the 1600s isn't likely to be of much help.

To search the surname list, click the **Searches** tab, then click the "RootsWeb Surname List (RSL)" link at the top of the page or go to <http://rsl.rootsweb.com> and click the "Search the RSL Database" link. In the search results, you

---

Surnames matching bobbitt

New entries are marked by a +, modified entries by a *, and expiring entries by an x. Clicking on the highlighted code words will give the name and address of the researcher who submitted the surname. (If no names are listed below this line, then none were found.)

Alternate Surnames (Click for a detailed list of alternates)

See the bobbitt resource page for more searches

You might have to scroll left or right to view all of the information

Surname	From	To	Migration	Submitter	Comment
Bobbitt	1600	now	Sommerset, Eng>NFLD>QC, CAN	ch1953	William and brother Thomas to Quebec's Lower North Shore. William settled Harrington, Thomas at Mutton Bay
Bobbitt	1600's	now	GLA,WLS>VA>KY>IN>,USA	arleneh	From William & Joanna in VA to James Henderson & Talitha in Pulaski Co KY
Bobbitt	1600's	Now	VI>KY	Beth1965	
Bobbitt	1620	----	ENG>USA	bstapley	
Bobbitt	1620	1880	Glamorganshire,WLS>VA>KY>IL	elamkely	
Bobbitt	1624	Current	GLA,WLS>VA>NC>SC>TN>ARK	TLaepple	
Bobbitt	1645	1950	WLS>VA>NC>TX,USA	daustin1	
Bobbitt	1645	c1800	WLS>VA,USA	woodlyn	
Bobbitt	1645	1846	WLS>VA	jet77	
Bobbitt	1645	now	GlamorganCo,WLS>Vidalia, GA	surfbird	GlamorganCo,WLS>VA>NC>SC>Vidalia GA
Bobbitt	1649	now	GLA>WLS>VA>NC,USA	kewltoy	
Bobbitt	1649	----	WLS>VA>KY,USA	jshubert	
Bobbitt	1649	1809	WLS>VA>NC>KY,USA	mickeya	
Bobbitt	1649	1970	VA>KY>IA,USA	younkin	

Next

Add your Surnames to the RSL

Surname *(required)*
bobbitt
Use surname;surname to see submitters researching both surnames

Location *(optional)*
Enter province, state or country abbreviation

Select type of search: ⦿ Surname ○ Soundex ○ Metaphone
Soundex and Metaphone are for sounds like matches

Updated during period: ⦿ Any ○ Last Week ○ Last Month ○ Last Two Months

[Submit] [Reset]

Entries for the BOBBITT surname in the RootsWeb Surname List

will see a "Submitter" column. This column shows you the ID of the individual who submitted the surname. Click on the submitter's ID to see his or her name, e-mail address, and sometimes his or her postal address.

> Note: You may find that some e-mail addresses don't work. The e-mail addresses for all "Currently Active" users have been verified within the last twelve months, but people often change their e-mail addresses and sometimes forget to update their information here. If you are unable to contact the submitter, you may want to submit your own surname information on RSL; you can also post information on a surname message board or mailing list. (For more information on mailing lists, see page 55. For more information on message boards, see page 37.)

To submit your own family surnames to RSL so that others can contact you, go to <http://rsl.rootsweb.com/cgi-bin/rsledit.cgi>.

The ROOTS-L Library

This online library contains hundreds of articles, bibliographies, guides, and other resources on a variety of family history topics, including a fabulous collection devoted to obtaining vital records, book lists from the Library of Congress, genealogy terms and definitions, and guides of useful tips for the beginning family historian. Some fun and interesting finds include:

- *Old Disease Names and Their Modern Definitions.* Did you ever wonder what that death certificate meant when it said your great-grandmother died of "dropsy?" You'll be interested to know this is likely the modern equivalent of congestive heart failure.

<http://ftp.rootsweb.com/pub/roots-l/genealog/genealog. disease1>

- *Guide for Interviewing Family Members.* If you are planning on recording an oral history of someone in the family, you can access and print this handy list of questions to ask.

<http://ftp.rootsweb.com/pub/roots-l/genealog/genealog.intrview>

- *Members of the Jesse James Gang.* You can find out who Jesse James's partners in crime were and also where they ended up.

<http://ftp.rootsweb.com/pub/roots-l/genealog/genealog. jjames1>

- *Quaker Abbreviations.* Have a Quaker in the family tree? This document of Quaker terms will explain the confusing abbreviations and phrases you might find in their records.

<http://ftp.rootsweb.com/pub/roots-l/genealog/genealog.quaker>

But to truly appreciate the great resources in this library you will have to explore it for yourself at <http://www.rootsweb. com/roots-l/filelist.html>.

Add-a-Link

If you, or an organization you belong to, have created a genealogy-related website that is not hosted by RootsWeb, you can link the website to RootsWeb so that it will be included in search results. To link your site to RootsWeb, go to the homepage and find the "Other Tools and Resources" section, then click the "Add A Link" link or go to <http://resources. rootsweb.com/~rootslink/addlink.html>.

What's New?

If you want to take a quick look at the new databases, mailing lists, and websites that have been added to RootsWeb in past weeks, check out the What's New page. Go to the homepage, find the "Getting Started" section, and click the "What's New" link or go to <http://whatsnew.rootsweb.com>.

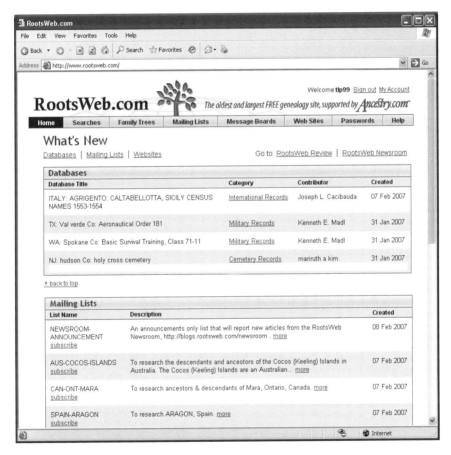

The What's New page lists new additions to the databases, mailing lists, and websites.

The Newsroom

The Newsroom is a forum for RootsWeb staff to tell you about new features, fixes to technical problems, and upcoming tools on the site. You'll want to check back often to see the latest updates to the site. One great feature of the Newsroom is the ability for you to add your own comments on any of the improvements and changes. Underneath each article or notice, you'll see a "Comments" link. Simply click the link to let other members and RootsWeb staff know what you think.

You can access the Newsroom on the homepage. Find the "Getting Started" section, and click the "RootsWeb Newsroom" link or go to <http://blogs.rootsweb.com/newsroom>.

The Newsroom

Alone
No Longer

By Sarah Feuerstein,
RootsWeb User

My husband's mother and her two sisters were in hiding in a village in Romania during the war [WWII]. As far as they knew, the rest of their family, all the SCHONZWEIGs who lived in Oradea and the surrounding areas, had disappeared. But they married and happily established families. Eventually they all moved to Israel.

A few years ago, I decided to put our genealogical data up on the Web. We got an e-mail from a woman in Israel saying that she seemed to have discovered her great-grandfather and great-great-grandfather on our family tree. After a flurry of exchanges we clarified all the details and the connection was made.

When we talked on the phone, tears were flowing as we found out that her father thought himself the only survivor of the SCHONZWEIG family, immigrated to Israel, changed his name, married, and had her—his only child. Being quite aged, he died when his daughter was still young. Now the daughter, reaching her middle age, was wondering if there were any SCHONZWEIGs at all in the world or if she was completely alone. Just as a test, she put the name into Google and, lo and behold, the first thing it brought up was our genealogical data and the names of her ancestors.

As a result of our e-mails and phone conversations she now has a decent-sized list of third cousins with their children and grandchildren to contact, which she did, and the family is planning a grand get-together in the coming weeks to welcome the lost cousin who is alone no longer.

Help:
Just a Click Away

As you explore RootsWeb, you may find that you need help navigating around the website or you may have questions about using a specific feature. RootsWeb has a HelpDesk to answer your questions. To access HelpDesk resources, simply click the Help tab.

Like most of RootsWeb, the HelpDesk is staffed by volunteers. These dedicated people work hard to ensure that most questions are answered the same day, and sometimes within hours—even on holidays and weekends.

The HelpDesk volunteers are happy to help you learn to use RootsWeb resources, but they cannot help you find your ancestors. Here are some things the HelpDesk can do for you:

- Answer questions about RootsWeb and its services and resources.

- Help you troubleshoot technical problems on the RootsWeb site.

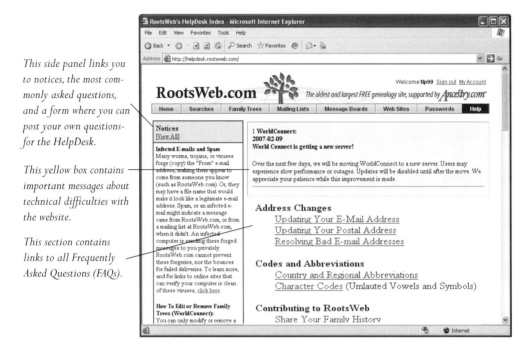

This side panel links you to notices, the most commonly asked questions, and a form where you can post your own questions—for the HelpDesk.

This yellow box contains important messages about technical difficulties with the website.

This section contains links to all Frequently Asked Questions (FAQs).

The HelpDesk homepage

Here are some things that the HelpDesk cannot do for you:

- Do your genealogical research for you. (Why spoil your fun?)

- Troubleshoot problems with your software, hardware, or Internet connection.

- Connect you with the person who is handling your immigration paperwork for your move from Kenya to Ethiopia.

- Find your first love—forty years after the fact.

- Identify the man with his arm around your granny in an old photo.

- Tell you how long it will take to do this "genealogy stuff."

- Verify that the "antique" you found is real—or tell you what it is worth.

- Force people to be nice or to respond to your e-mails and message board posts.

Announcements and Notifications

When you click on the **Help** tab, the first thing you will notice at the top of the Help page is a large yellow box. This box contains important messages about technical problems and website errors and is updated regularly. Do not contact the HelpDesk about a problem that is already listed here—these are all issues that the RootsWeb staff is aware of and are in the process of fixing.

In addition to these technical notices, RootsWeb includes a "newsroom." The Newsroom includes updates about new features, fixes to technical problems, and more. For more information, see page 96.

Frequently Asked Questions (FAQs)

Over the years, the HelpDesk has been asked thousands and thousands of questions. The staff has gathered the most common questions—and their answers—and has grouped them in categories on the main Help page. You will find information on all RootsWeb features, everything from mailing lists to RootsWeb member accounts. Before you submit your own questions to the HelpDesk, make sure you use this great resource; your problem may have already been solved.

To browse the FAQs, click the **Help** tab. Then, scroll through the different help topics. Click the link that most closely resembles your question's topic. Each link contains a a variety of resources; you may find step-by-step instructions, terms and definitions, or related help pages.

Contacting the HelpDesk

If you've reviewed all the Help topics and the FAQs available at the HelpDesk, and you still can't find an answer to your problem or question, you can send a e-mail request to the HelpDesk. To create a request, you need to fill out a specific form. Click the "HelpDesk" link that is located on the bottom, left-hand side of the Help page in the "Still Need Help?" box or you can access the request form directly by visiting <http:// helpdesk.rootsweb.com/form1.html>. For best results, follow these guidelines when submitting a question:

- Do not post requests for personal genealogical research help; your request will not be answered.

- Be sure to include the program, feature, or database you are inquiring about, and include the Web address (if possible). If the problem pertains to a mailing list or a message board, please be specific as to which one. For WorldConnect family trees, provide details, such as the tree's user code.

- Do not use angle brackets (< >) in your message. The programs used by the HelpDesk prevent the staff from reading any text that is included in angle brackets.

- If you are having trouble submitting the Help form, it might be because of the firewall security program you are using on your computer; turn off your security program and resubmit the form. Don't forget to turn the program on again when you're done.

Still Need Help?

If you've checked the resources shown here, and you still have a question or problem, then please post a message with our HelpDesk.

Please take a moment to check the help pages listed on this page before posting on the message board.

If your question concerns a specific website, you should contact the webmaster for that site. Contents of the individual sites are the responsibility of the webmasters, not RootsWeb.com.

Click the "HelpDesk" link to access a HelpDesk request form.

A Family Picture Finds a New Home

By D. Lou Ritter,
RootsWeb User

I live in Michigan and my paternal Scottish MUNRO ancestors came from Scotland to Ontario, Canada, in about 1827. Last fall I received an e-mail from a woman in Missouri who had purchased a composite family picture at an antique store, not because she had a family connection, but just because she liked it. However, she was curious about the picture and went online to learn about the names mentioned on the photo.

She found all of the names in a family tree that I had posted on RootsWeb. I had no known connections to Missouri, but said I would be interested in seeing the pictures if she could e-mail them to me. Several months passed and I forgot about the contact. Then, one day, an e-mail arrived with digital images attached.

It turned out that this composite family picture was of my second great-grandfather, his seven siblings, and all of their spouses. I had seen three of the images before, so I was sure about the connection. We negotiated my purchase of the picture from her and I have since had the images all professionally scanned, which will protect them and makes it possible to share the pictures with cousins far and wide.

I am overwhelmed that I was so fortunate to be able to possess these images of sixteen people who lived in the mid-nineteenth century. I am now having the picture re-framed, and it will hang over my computer for daily inspiration.

Chapter 9

My Account and Passwords

Although you don't have to be a registered member of RootsWeb to do many tasks on the site—search the message boards, subscribe to a mailing list, or browse the family trees—you *must* be a registered member to post messages to the boards, add a tree to WorldConnect, submit databases, and much more.

Creating a member account is simple *and* free so there's no reason not to join and start enjoying all the benefits of being a RootsWeb member. Keep all your e-mail addresses current so others can locate you; manage all your favorite features and subscriptions from one centralized location; and create a public profile so other RootsWeb members who share your interests can contact you.

If you aren't already registered, you can create a new member account by clicking the "Sign in" link at the top, right-hand side of any RootsWeb page or by going to <https://secure.rootsweb.com/rweb/accountinfo.aspx?ti.si=3&ctype=3>.

My Account

You can access your account at any time by clicking the "My Account" link available at the top, right-hand side of any RootsWeb page. Your account gives you one central location for managing all your activities on RootsWeb and also makes it easier for you to update your personal information such as adding a new e-mail address.

The Personal Information section on the My Account page lets you update your member name and e-mail address and

Shows a list of all your WorldConnect trees, mailing lists, and links you to any lists you administer.

Click a link to update your member account information, e-mail addresses, or public profile.

Click here to subscribe or unsubscribe from newsletters.

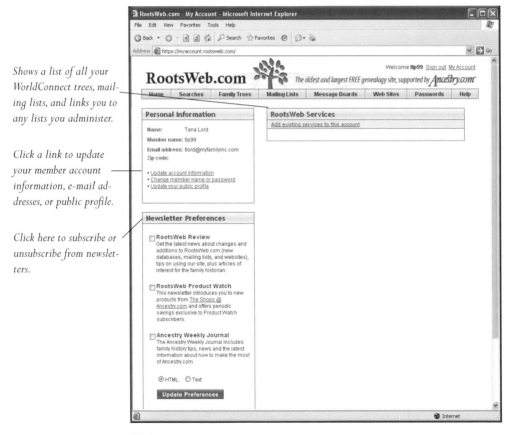

My Account

your public profile that is attached to your public posts. (For more information on public profiles, see page 50.)

> Note: When you add information to the site (for example, if you post a message on the message boards, add an entry to the RootsWeb Surname List, or add a tree to WorldConnect), the member name and e-mail address in your member account may be publicly viewable to identify you in connection with these posts. If you do not want others to know your full name, you may want to select a shorthand version of your name, a nickname, or some other term to serve as your Member Name.

The Newsletter Preferences section lets you determine which e-mail newsletters you want to receive and whether you receive them in HTML or text formats. The three newsletters you can receive are the *RootsWeb Review*, the *RootsWeb Product Watch*, and the *Ancestry Weekly Journal*.

The third section, RootsWeb Services, links you to features such as your WorldConnect family trees, your Post-ems, and personalized mailing lists. If you are the administrator of a message board, a link to both the message board and the administration tools will also be listed in this section.

Working with Passwords

In order to use many features on RootsWeb, you must become a registered user of the site using an e-mail address and password. If you ever forget your password, you can have it sent to your e-mail address.

To retrieve a forgotten password, click the **Passwords** tab. Enter your registered e-mail address; then, select the site features you need passwords for—the passwords will be e-mailed to the address you specified. If you've used several different e-mail addresses, you may need to repeat this process several times, once for each address.

Passwords homepage

Index

Index

About the Authors

Myra Vanderpool Gormley, CG

Myra is a certified genealogist and a retired syndicated columnist and feature writer for the Los Angeles Times Syndicate. She has written three books and more than a thousand articles on the subject of genealogy. She served as an editor of *RootsWeb Review* from 1998 to 2007. Among her awards are the DAR Continental Congress Special Recognition Award and the National Genealogical Society's Award of Merit for distinguished work in genealogy.

Tana Pedersen Lord

Tana has been writing and editing in the technology industry more than ten years. In that time, she has earned several awards for her writing including the Distinguished Technical Communication award from the Society for Technical Communication. She is currently Editorial Manager for The Generations Network™, a contributing editor to *Ancestry* Magazine, and author of *The Official Guide to Family Tree Maker 2006*.